A

THE NEON MYTHS

Colin Tan

Copyright © 2021 Colin Tan
All rights reserved.
ISBN: 9798495449763

Prologue

Neon Primus
What you call consciousness,
conceals the location of the centre of all things,
and what you call time,
is a thought crime.
At the centre of all things,
something tries to remember.
It tries to remember its name.
It tries to remember its appearance.
It tries to remember emotion.
It tries to remember the shape of a soul.
And every time it does,
a new life is born.
And when it finally remembers,
all life will end,
and you will be remembered as something else.
Your world changes in some small way,
every time you forget.
And life begins again in some small way,
every time you remember.
Such is the way of sentient things,
each day the world remembers the sun,
as you must remember yourself,
until all is forgotten.

Book One

The City of Lost Shadows

I Lost My Shadow In An Alley

I went there, where
concrete grows thicker
than trees
and neon lights float
like fruit
without branches.

Imaginings complete a view
without the 4k of the sun,
and with no vanishing
point in this scene,
I had to sacrifice for
perspective.

In the morning I was blind,
without my shadow,
I could not see where,
the sun did shine.

The City of Lost Shadows

There are no streets just alleys.
There is no sun just a moon,
and the only light is its reflection in neon bloom.
There is no illusion in the perspective of a dead end,
as every corner vanishes to a point,
and a fog of shattered hearts,
smokes every joint.

I was not born here
and I will not die here.
I have always been here,
faded and afraid,
jaded and unmade.
The family album in which,
you confined my images, is,
a lie.
They were never a when,
they have always been,
a why.
I was not born there,
and I will not die there,
I seek no pole of negatives.

On one street is a karaoke bar where,
in a private room,
you can only whisper to your childhood,
and scream at your broken heart.
From nineteen ninety-five you can redefine,
any fear with a bucket of a beer
and a sign on the wall says
"experience is a loaded question,
that freedom is the answer to."

There is a lady on a corner,
under a streetlight all night.
She was not born there,
and she will not die there,
but she is often assumed to be there,
when all is not right.
Make an assumption of her curve,
and you will find the sharp point of the corner,
for it is only right to be at right angles,
with any man's daughter.

I sacrificed my shadow,
many moons ago,
to walk with feet that could never be told,
where to go,
because I wanted to forget,
that my heart burns in the sun,
where somebody I love,
smiles with another one.

We will never see an eclipse here,
but when it rains,
we smile as we cry,
when it rains,
we all look up to the sky.

Karaoke

In this place the breeze commits a relational transgression as it blows
and all that glitters is reflections of light in the rain.
I booked a room to sing Tony Bennett at the top of my lungs,
and scream at the absurdity of breathing with no purpose,
but alas got lost in contemplation and imagining, creating,
the face of a person who makes irrelevant and absurd music videos,
for shadowless people to sing along to.
Perhaps this is how we all came into existence,
and so, I found an answer of some sorts.

Outside I heard a wailing and beheld her on the corner.
Outside my heart was failing at the lament of some man's daughter.
The breeze carried her tears horizontally into the headlights,
and as I caught the dance of the light and the water,
the movement in that moment only brief,
made me notice my breath and ignore my grief.

The car did not stop it carried on,
the world does not stop it carries on,
for that is the way of things,
that is how it goes for non-living things.
And in the next moment,
the mound of her,
the shape of her,
a Bauhuas barrow on the tarmac,
stole my breath away,
as the contents of her bag rolled across the road,
and fled the scene.

My next breath came with a scream,
not unlike that which a baby makes for the first time,
not unlike the sound of a creature on borrowed time.
I hurried to her shape and fell to my knees,
to damp and stone and the sound of the breeze.
I peeled open her long dark coat to shock and horror,
there was nobody or no person under its cover.
I prayed to no God that I was dreaming,
and my tears lost all meaning,
as the breeze carried them sideways into the lights.
I reflected on life as another one of those nights,
and tried to imagine songs which would fit such a scene,
and the face of who may sing along to such a dream.

J

The Abstinence From Perspective

She grew up in the corner house,
but now the plaster had grown into dust,
ashen and faux pollen,
and the wire had faded into rust,
ration and slow fallen.
The sound of a crackled cackle,
the gift of reservation that was electric,
is now an anthem she no longer sings.

The taste of the poppy seeds brewed into tea for the children,
to inspire laughter at the static of grey and white on the screen,
still lingers however, forever a lingering scene.
Sour to begin with and the sweetest to end with,
the bitterest of tickles to a delight of dreams.
Only endings ever truly begin,
and a journey of in between is always relative,
and like me she found more perspective,
in the dead ends of alleyways.

And so it may have been years or only minutes,
that she had danced in the club near the bar,
next to a pole of a stem,
and under petals of neon flickers.
Oh, how electric tickles,
and hearts beat static fickle.

The shadows of shapes and crimson eyes,
constantly drooled and fooled,
and spoke of betrothment in lies,
as the beer mats drowned to mush without rush.
For whether it had been minutes or years,

K

she had forever abstained,
to masturbate is to celebrate,
to celibate and to castigate,
a divination in binarization.

Like the poppy seeds,
the bitterness of my beginnings,
sought the sweetness of her endings,
of any shape and form she brought to being,
and so I continued my search for meaning.

I trembled as she danced for me,
I quivered as she moved for me,
until she smiled and she asked me,
how it was it came to be?
There was no answer that I could see,
"Yet you are here now,"
she said to me,
"and therefore, you have come to be."
A tear formed in my nose as I closed,
my eyes to absorb the form of her,
and then I returned to her.
"Is this a woman you see before you?
Your point angled toward my hands?"
"I cannot answer with my eyes or my hands,
I believe I saw a woman earlier,
befall a terrible accident of glass of steel,
but there was no form to feel,
no body to discover under the cover,
of her coat that was left on the street,
alas a lady any sort I have yet to meet."

"You need not lament for the lost,
the shadow that you have forgot,
and in this city my form matters not.
But know this,
your hands will be forever lonely here,
if they only know your point my dear."

"But I only know what I have been told,
I only know what I have been sold,
that it is wrong to hold another like my own."

"A life alone is a life of none and only one,
will you ever perceive despite how many times you breathe,
and remember,
whatever you believe,
I can imagine better."

At once I became his and hers and hers and his,
in a minute of perspective or a year with respective,
for I began at the end,
and my end had just begun.

Polarised

A corner house
of stale plaster and protest wire.
The shadows outside forget the sun,
the shadows inside are no one.
Another corner an achromatic cat abstains grey,
poised paw upon the pavement cracks.
Behind him the laughter of steel bicycle spokes
as the children lose their limbs to tell jokes.
Photographs purvey the mind monochromatic meanderings,
and poetry is claimed by the arrogance of an image that you remember.
I am prompted to prompt myself and need not a poke from behind your eyes.
I will abstain thoughts like lies and stroke this cat until I perceive a pussy sound,
you my friend are now hearing what I found.
My life today is an album of polaroids,
because that is all you will remember.
I sat and watched two old ladies in a coffee shop crinkle their lips and stroke their hips,
and say absolutely nothing, does this mean that they mean, nothing?
They made no sound at all as if someone outside turned off the light
and if I could talk to them I might,
not,

MIGHT

not

might

NOT.

N

This is a life in polaroid,
and this is the lie of colours filtered.

FOCUS.

0

The Street Behind You

The house on the corner is forever silent,
muted by the sound of a family who cannot sleep.
In a garage a man plays the drums on empty paint cans,
as his wife watches the bedroom walls peel and blister.
Rain falls upwards as it pours,
and umbrellas instil fear into children.
There is a virgin who binges on crime documentaries,
knowing only an arousal of blood,
and when the wind blows you can hear the groans
of the land this street was built upon.
Rodents and other things gossip at night,
they mock ethnicity and despise authenticity
as bats mourn fallen leaves with their wings,
to eventually settle upon neon fruit.
This is the street behind you,
where your memories become pictures to repaint
and love is a jigsawed collage.

The Smell of Humans

the conversation rises
like the water in the bath
and then falls away
just as fast
sinking
I am
into the wholes
of her lies
her eyes
a disguise
of being high

the DJ proclaims
that there is no human smell in this club
and as the girls continue to dance
I realise
senses have departed
a disguise
of the broken hearted

she smiles a reflection of neon
if she ate me alive
I am sure that my skin would tan
and there is no sun
or human smell
in this club
some of us long to be eaten alive
to be appear as fresh meat and not frozen
what kind of life do we lead
if death is the only evidence of being alive
if our death proves we never tried?

Q

nothing we say
or do
appears strange in the dark
and so we all find comfort
in blankets of the heart
we constantly talk of closure
yet fear such exposure
to expose but not be exposed
is a flaw in the human condition
her smile is exposed
because she knows
she has caught me
wide open
in this space
I will dream of that face
when the lights come on
and kiss
no one, not one

Gary

You breathe in
and forget to breath out
because it all feels so fucking,
wonderful.

Your palm strokes your thigh
and it feels like your skin,
has felt itself for the very first time.
It itches into silk and etches into warmth,
instantly
and now you cannot stop,
touching yourself,
for a minute,
or an hour.
It is hard to tell when your heart beats
the minutes and
you have lost track of yourself.

A hand smashed into your face last week,
and your tears hit the ground like broken glass,
but none of that matters anymore.
For a second or perhaps a minute,
this thought runs through your head
that none of that really matters,
you do not really matter,
you do not want to matter,
and perhaps nothing at all matters.
So you smile for a while,
eyes closed and mind reposed in fragments,
because in that second or minute,
you find this notion,
hilarious,

and none of this really matters.

Heat rises up through your body like bath water
and a booming bass beat
peelsyourpulsebackintoanegngagedtoneabusytoneotherwise,
reposed.

Breathe.

A kaleidoscope of fucking fragments
which feel so fucking,
wonderful.

Fuck.

You had sex yesterday
that only lasted minutes,
but this night will go on for seconds,
minutes,
and hours and every inch of you,
skin,
hair,
the sweat shimmering on your face,
will go away and come back again,
a million times before then.

You took a pill,
or two,
or three,
and at some point tomorrow,
the world will throw you up again.
But right now,
none of that really matters.
Right now,
you do not need to matter
and that is fucking,
wonderful.

The Jazz Club

Smoke sinks slowly, lingers like the dream mist,
shadows left on the eyes so late it is morning.
The sound of warmth, thumbs on bass strings melt,
like fingers in chocolate,
nothing melts like a finger,
in chocolate.

The scar on the eyebrow hides how his eyes see the notes,
dancing to the crystal clink of fingernails on ivory,
and this black and white ain't binary.
The trumpet breathes and fills her lungs,
the trumpet breathes and fills her lungs,
the strumpet bleeds and rips her tongue
and then she finds her voice,
she swallows,
she swallows,
this choice,
for her voice,
and the repetition bleats the beat.

A Picasso melts on the far wall,
but nobody cares,
time ticks to an offbeat now,
because nobody cares.
Music is no metaphor if you can't feel what you hear,
and words say nothing when you can't hear what you feel,
hearing feeling meaning and being need the tempo,
you know,
that's just the way it is,
it ain't Picasso,
you know.

Outside.
Outside,
the rain dances down, diagonals and diameters,
trickling to ripples down the stairs as the sound,
as the sound,
man,
oh man,
the sound,
the sound man,
writes his song.
The cat the cat the cat laughs
oh he laughs at why he laughs.
It's cooler than grinning,
much cooler than grinning,
because the music is playing
for a note or two,
this moment with you.

One.
Two.
Three.
Four.

Four.
   One.
 Three.
    Two.
       Four.
         One.
     Three.
       Two.

This is the sound of you,
in a moment of you.

w

Humpback

The bar was a traffic jam and felt no wider than the length of his arms, because on some nights that is all the world is. Her arms were covered with needle tracks in the shape of names, and his were not long enough to hold onto her.

Her words tore chunks out of his flesh, as if his bones were a treasure to be scavenged. The tide had gone out and left his stranded carcass behind. He had nothing to say, like the sound of waves, such questions often go unanswered.

Tears, sometimes, are pointless, but like many things they will fall anyway because of gravity, and so hers fell like rain onto the sea, instantly forgotten.

In the morning the hangover pecked at what was left of him and a stone hit his bedroom window to see if anybody was home. He lay still like a withered piece of driftwood, dried out with memories of a tide.

Not too far away two children laughed on the beach and skipped stones across the water as the sun lit up their eyes. The waves sounded different that morning, punctuated by the flip flip plip plop of the stones.

The Point

The corners of this room define my existence from nine to nine,
angles converged to a point and black and white tiles of binary design.
There is no giving in derision,
and so it is fitting to be imprisoned so,
in this room and within,
safe in gloom and the dim.

With every breath I remember,
I close my eyes to rediscover to repaint,
every colour and hue of her,
every shimmer and screw of her,
and I fall apart like metal and glass in a car crash,
every time my mind leads me to the last time,
I ever saw her face,
lifeless and sallow,
dead in dreams of tomorrow.

And each time I scream the sharp needle nurse gleams,
she comes,
oh she comes,
to bring sleep to all my dreams.
Each time my eyelids sink,
I see the lies of my eyes,
her face is not hers
her name is not hers
I am given this image to encumber,
and drown in medicated slumber.

I cannot be here,
I cannot breath here,
in this place or this time,
in this body or this mind.

At some needled point,
in some thought or moment.
My mind,
and my heart,
choose to depart,
this space beyond my eyes.
And yet in this room I may still lay,
I only saw the face of my love,
on the shape of the nurse today
and I smiled before the needle blame,
as I died before my freedom came.

The Scenic Route

On a street not unlike the one close to you,
a couple hold hands,
footsteps in sync,
their hearts beat a discrepant echo.
One of them looks not unlike yourself and the other,
looks like somebody you wish you could remember.
Their lips move to mime memories of words they never said,
and the wind,
like a magpie steals the sound,
neither whisper nor silver to be found.
This could be the last time somebody dreams of you,
or the first time somebody remembers you.
On this street,
time is just a word which,
like any other,
changes nothing without meaning,
just like the air in your lungs,
that you don't remember breathing.

AA

The Flood

The sun rose like the bruise on my arm
and the origin of both is a mystery to me.
I imagine something like pain to the touch
but like the shape of a cloud, something eludes me.
Outside the city drowned under a foot of water
and I waited barefoot and cool on the corner,
carrying my shoes like a gift to my former life,
for a black bus to burrow towards me like a blunt knife,
leaving a trail of shimmering spectrums,
diesel leaks and exhaust bubbles,
ripple sweeps and discoursed troubles.

It was a fine day to be alive,
and an even better day to go outside.
The driver was of a gaseous form,
a body of smoke beneath a uniform.
To perceive each emblem of an institution,
as a dereliction of a constitution
is a sign of such times where only the truth rhymes,
and hope is a forgotten street name.

I staggered towards a seat opposite a woman at the rear,
and I as I got near I became comatose with fear.
She was the unform of a non-uniform female form,
and the most striking shape my eyes have ever seen,
my eyelids screamed to close to escape such a dream.
A short black bob that enslaved the night,
with eyes distorted across her brow
into pink and blue and yellow,
red and black burning white.
Her mind beyond was a rainbow I imagined,
and her lips where the most human thing I could ever perceive,

BB

rouge red crimson damson dripping with blood that cannot deceive.
I should have been afraid,
I should have been terrified,
I should have run away
and felt petrified,
but she looked at me.
She saw me,
and me she smiled,
and until that day
I had never felt alive.

Her dress was made of canvas,
and flecked with oils.
I wore only my flesh,
and a confusion of bones,
my skeleton of ossein
devoid of objectivity.

"Where are you going?"
I asked and she just smiled.
"I want to leave this place,"
I said completely beguiled.
The bus drifted to a halt and signalled the end of
this double deckered game of checkers.

CC

Her hand melted around mine and set like wax
as she me lead outside and I saw that we had departed,
at the very same spot our journey started.
I realised had forgotten my shoes,
such was the life I was about to choose.
Around her feet colours leaked into the water,
it rose and rose as a flower grows,
and her hand and her smile kept me planted.
I did not fear being unable to breathe,
if a bird swims or a fish flies,
the matter is only perspective,
her smile and colours had given me a directive.

As the water reached her lips she placed my hands on her hips
and all around the city continued to drown.
I watched in awe as the last bubble of air tickled my face,
and the colours she had for eyes dissolved like paint,
to reveal her face and the true nature of this place
and every inch of me succumbed to her distraint.
I resolved to dissolve into every last drop of her,
and find ecstasy on becoming nothing,
the beauty in being alive and nothing,
and accepting that there is nothing,
beyond this city of sunken things,
where only the fish have wings.

DD

Iris

When I think of the moon reflecting the light of the sun
and the mood of the planet I live on,
I think of my eyes and the light they let inside.
They see nothing unfiltered and so the mind of a sponge,
becomes a terrifying notion.
Up close the eyes look like a map of the universe,
at their centre a great black hole.
Each eye is unique they say and so,
machines can use them to tell people apart,
with no less understanding of the heart.
Perhaps eyes show the way to the soul,
perhaps our fingerprints map routes across the stars,
back to whence we came,
a place we dream to remember of.
I dreamt once and remembered once,
a tale of a city and a he and a she.
A tale of two people amongst many,
stuck in a place they tried to see what they could be.

Conversations, a background of static,
they could hear only the whisper of electric.
The streetlights traced ideas,
figments faded and forgotten,
and the only way to know the time,
was to count the cracks on the pavement.
She looked into his eyes,
to find what he saw,
even though experience told her,
that eyes only show reflections,
traffic lights of a mood.
That night they decided not to kiss,
but bite each other's lips,

to bleed out the cyan of Corinthians,
because there is only truth in lessons of pain.

In that city where,
a church has no roof,
and alleyways steal shadows,
people hold hands to feel to know,
that it is not a dream.
They look through the windows,
to see the side of the glass,
that only buffers their reflection at night.
Nothing is unfiltered,
not even the light of the sun and the moon.
This is why some men go mad,
in search of the truth,
and others beg on corners,
to buy a ticket to choose.

She always said love was the truth,
but it was a notion she read about,
that somebody else wrote about,
which entered her head,
like the light of the sun and the moon.
After that night they stopped making love,
because they no longer knew what it meant.

I dreamt about this place,
to remember this place.
I wrote about this place,
so that others may read of this place.
Dreaming is something we do with our eyes closed,
meaning is a room we look for behind doors closed.
And perhaps love is another place,
we can never find our way back to,
and perhaps the soul is a place,
we don't remember how to get to.

GG

The Broken Window

To the far-right corner of what you see,
is a broken window in this darkness,
jagged teeth of razor and grey.
You hold up your hand to its pale gloom,
to confirm the existence of fingers
but all you discern is a silhouette of a city skyline.

Anywhere is here and everywhere is there,
is that not how it feels,
some days?
A silence seethes,
a silence unsettles,
in moments like these,
your mind meddles.

Your heart dances like an electric harpsichord
and the throb and pulse in the rear of where,
you imagine your head sleeps is the chorister of this cloister
of logic that you are currently scurrying to.
To be anywhere, to be everywhere,
here and there but anywhere and everywhere but,
near,
there.

Two by two by two by four,
feet, arms and limbs.
Two by two for a door,
an area, a volume, the brim.
There are ways of seeing,
there are ways of being
and there are ways of feeling
to find more meaning.

HH

You now turn to the window again,
and hold up both of your hands
to touch a Rorschach smile
and wait a while,
until it frowns a triptych child.

There is no way out from no way in,
you could read Baudolino
or drink Faustino
and be none the wiser in such moments.
In such moments, sounds become more,
sounds become senses
and silence seethes,
silence unsettles softly,
silence seethes softly.

More meanings, more memories more momentary meanderings,
more murmurs, melodiously montaged making movements
in this space you are defining.
Here you now confide
in what little you recognise
to realise or actualise
a sense of where you are,
near or far to what you are.
Ask yourself when,
not why you are.
Ask yourself where,
not who you are.

The Red Shoes

Sleep.
A dream.
I hear the clatter of its hooves,
and wake with a clamour to the sound,
of jar lids stutter across the tiles.
I imagine a mess of pickles, sauces and powder,
and the chaos of the corporeal collage.
I find nothing but an empty pair of red shoes,
in the centre of the floor,
of the empty room,
and a tightly locked door,
that seals a question.

The train shunts and shutters,
the rain stutters in the gutters,
beyond this arterial serpent of steel and glass,
and I am denied the space of an egg,
in its carton of a carriage.
My arms cling to the handrail in the style of the accused,
knuckles white and bloodied palms,
as my body wriggles and writhes abused
by the proximity of bodies unknown and unwelcome,
underhand and underneath.

One space is empty.
One seat is empty.
A silhouette of lines and angles
where a pale light dangles,
to the floor and more,
an empty pair of red shoes,
and a choice nobody wished to choose.

JJ

The river babbles,
and a bluebird cackles over my head.
It twists itself into the gist of a horizon,
and I look for shadows on the bank but find none.
There is a bluebird above but a sky there is none,
no reflection on the water but my own,
just an idea of myself that I had once,
nothing more than a whimsical impulse.

Again I hear the clatter and clamour,
the stutter and mutter and I follow the sound,
but again and yet again,
there is only a pair of red shoes to be found.
Empty at the riverside,
with neither a trail nor footprint,
as if the earth and soil had lied,
or stole an impression to hide.

In the end I find myself,
at the very end I see myself,
on a bench of wood and moss.
A sound in the distance implies thunder,
whether a beckoning or a reckoning this weather,
is too far ahead or behind to perceive,
and so my eyes fall to this lie of a ground.
On the flesh of my bare feet I witness the attenuation,
and thinned declaration of my salmoned sanguine.
Perhaps it was not the ground but I,
that left neither trail nor print,
and nothing but a lie,
under this unseen sky.

KK

The Waiting Room

Such places are never truly on the square,
and so it was that I perceived many corners.
I felt as though I were seated in a polyhedron,
but perhaps I was nauseous,
and perhaps that was why I was there.

I was grateful for the grey cloth of the sofa,
my comportment cajoled.
I despise leather,
its song is uncomfortable,
the scars intolerable.

"What are you in for?"
I joked with the boy next to me,
offence is the best defence my young self often believed.
"My dreams disturb me,
I can barely shave the stubble of the sky,"
came his honest reply.

The lady opposite grunted,
"Are you okay?" I asked.
"It's just kicking, that's all."
"What are you having?"
"A baby."
"I meant are you having a boy or a girl?"
"I'm having baby."
The young boy chuckled,
and the belly of the woman appeared to reciprocate,
I was definitely nauseous and in need of escape.
"And how are you sir?"
I asked the elderly gentleman to my right.
"I need to talk to somebody."

"I see, are you here alone?"
"I've been alone for some time,
I haven't found my wife."
"Oh, I am truly sorry for your loss."
"I didn't lose her; I haven't found her."
"I misunderstood; I am sorry."
He grunted a reply and then slowly,
closed his eyes.

Having exhausted my energy for discourse,
I scanned the room for another distraction from the dimension,
of my surroundings.
A coffee table of mirrored glass emerged from below my feet,
its corners traces of light and promises,
memories and choices.

I discovered a magazine,
the title 'Portmanteau',
in shimmering gleam,
across a blank vacant front.
I discovered travel scenes in callous colours,
poems of monochromatic lovers,
and in the middle of all these,
a review of "On the Origin of Species."

MM

After some time or no time at all I finished the magazine,
and returned it to the glimmer and gleam.
Immediately a door opened,
and a figure in a blank white coat,
with a tattoo of a face,
spoke to me with unmoving lips,
its voice a spectrum of sound.
"You can go now," it said,
and so it was that my condition was jilted,
by such words unfiltered.

The Sky In The Matchbox

curled up in a hoodie for a pillow
eyes closed hiding and darkness wanting
sleep is a dream that taunts my soul like a taste of a drug
my mind drifts and random thoughts appear and I am not here
but dreams they are not and sleep this is not
and when I open my eyes my bed has departed
I am lying on a floor behind a burnt door
in a room I do not know
in a body I hardly know

the walls look familiar
but all mould looks the same
damp is a constant the world over
and penury is the name
of a street that never ends
where every house looks the same

I feel cold in bones wrapped in flesh too thin
and clothes as thin as the skin I am in
the silence is darker than the night
there is no sound despite the speckles of light
from outside that allow me to recall the memory of limbs
and try to leave this place
to discover the outside and living things

sallow grey floorboards
of ash and dust make no sound
I move in a song of silence
I can barely see
and choke on the smell
of a depicted reality

this is a building of broken windows and locked doors
of crackling wires and terrified lights
the pervasive absence of sound
dampens my heart and I have no proof
of blood in my veins
as my very heart
has forgotten my name

I need to breath
I want to see the sky
I want to leave
to be outside
a simple life
would be outside
under the sky
where I can see the lights
and hear the sounds
I find stairs and climb
I go around and around
and head upside from down
yet still hear not a sound

this helix twists
me around damp
dust and bricks
plaster is grey and there is ash greyer still
and night is never black enough
to steal away a chill
of a forgotten dream

there is no end to this climb
no roof or sky I find
the way out eludes me
like the idea of sleep it taunts me

until I crumble into a corner on the stairs
and I can no longer see a way up or down
my eyes begin to fail me as I look for a door
I can barely make out a shape on the floor
I reach out with my hand to feel the smooth surface and rough sides
of a mouldy matchbox and I smile
it feels like a life I imagine I had
and the shape of a dream I once had

in the dimming embers of my fading strength
I shake it to hear a sound
but no way to wake is found
I hear nothing and open the box
to find burnt matches and a dream of a cloud
a lump of cotton wool that makes no sound
my arms fall as far and slow as my eyelids
and I return to a dream of fire all around

QQ

A Visit To The Gallery

the centrepiece
of this room at least is
'an installation by strawmen'
humanoid lines contorted into non-human shapes
the twisted angles of those in narcotic necrophilia
and soporific slumber
the skylight prostrates to the moonlight and filters
the chicken wire twisted frames and hessian skin
into dreams that kept Rorschach awake as a child

in one corner on the wall
language languishes in letters
neither black nor white
on neither canvas nor papyrus
in the form of a poem called
'clitoris tongue'

a landscape opposite
implies the ocean and a line
stretched to a perspective
that comes in waves
and departs with the tide
I recall a dream
and I holiday I had
as a child
and read
'on the horizon'

'a chart of home'
in another corner

RR

smashed glass
and wood and things
are plotted out to an unseen axis
on the floor is a fixed point
from which point
and at which angle
the pieces line up in my vision
and I perceive a table and things
and with a slight deviation
a scatter of memories again

the room ahead is in darkness until
it drowns me in light and sound
it is difficult to breath until I cough
and expel silence from my lungs
a field of flickers of yellow
pink, cyan and magenta
stroboscopically suspended in soundseams
it seems
threads that we only imagine
I pass through them like a ghost
and enter the next room having left
an unknown piece of me behind
this was 'the tethering of fireflies'

before me lies
'a form of desire'
a circular pool
consonated with concentric ripples
that intermittently catch a reflection
of the light behind my eyes
here and only here
have I experienced
the solubility of the self
and all anagrams of anxiety

at last again
alas again
I wait outside
on the cold steps of waking
for a rendezvous with déjà vu
and a hand to hold and walk through
the gallery unseen by others
but I am ambushed by an opening of my eyes
my arm flops around like
a cuttlefish corpse
and as the tingling taunts my flesh
the first thought I have
is whether I have touched death
or held the hand of my consciousness

Burnt

there are dreams folded neatly
into fingernail size envelopes of cotton
and burnt as offerings to the nameless
as a pale woman devours a field of lemon balm
she only smells when she sleeps or sleeps when she smells
her thoughts all too often two steps far removed from mint
in the glint of her eyes is a hint, a disguise
of a notion or a whim
but this sort of lemon is not sharp enough
to pierce your hungry skin

such truths like some photographs
can only be developed in dark rooms
corner less and boundless
volumized in darkness
wherein such places
a whisper or a voice travels at the same rate
and a moment captured knows not its fate

when dealt enough pain we bleed
and a substance of love we need
yet it beats not within us
this whim, this notion of a heart
is a dream to us
and so we burn offerings
to the nameless
and think in the dark
of whims like the heart
content, and shameless
human, and formless

UU

The Unmaking

he became
an unmade man
an unkempt man
an unironed tee shirt of a man
an unshaven, bed unmade independent man
for he made all of these things, entirely within
for all making begins within
he was independent of the sound and din
he was never unloved
but rarely understood
and rarely understood love in being not quite unloving
being unmade in this readymade land of misunderstanding
being unheard and unseen and unfelt
he then became unhearing by removing his ears
he became unseeing by burning his eyes
he became unfeeling by removing his limbs
and eventually he became unambiguous
and devoid of ambiguity
he began to remake himself from within
and outside remained the sound and the din
his bed remained forever unmade
and he slept quite soundly within

The Love Hotel

signboards of carnival colours drift and float outside
parading their propositions
like lotus plants on a concrete pond
they ripple and flutter ever so slightly so sweetly
with each desire and dream
of those who wander in from outside
like hungry insects
people predators prey
dirty puddles and smoke stained troubles

Room 101: Loyalty
There is no colour in this room,
just contrasting shades, tones and shadow,
an absence of hue creates the mood.
Mariko lies on the bed,
her bare skin the lightest shade in the room,
her hair the darkest bloom.
Belly down her nipples tease the sheets,
and her toes curl back and upwards,
into the dancing shadows of the ceiling fan.
She browses through a lingerie catalogue,
licks her fingers and teases the corners of the pages.
She cannot imagine herself in another pair of knickers,
whilst entertaining others between her legs,
and so naked and ready she must be.
To desire black lace whilst wearing white lace is a disgrace,
and that is always how it should be.

ww

Room 204: A Choice
The bath is too hot it reprimands,
hotter than the blood in his veins,
and so his mind becomes feint.
The water overflows ever so slowy,
but he cares not.
He imagines as he ebbs away,
that the essence of him,
will be diluted and that is apt,
for he will be forgot.
He imagines he is sweating,
but he is too wet to notice,
too hot to focus,
and this is apt,
for he will be forgot.
The razor blade rests on the side,
and he catches the reflection of his eyes,
the eyes he forgot,
and in shock and recall
his finger he cuts,
on the paper of the note,
he is to leave behind.
He bleeds,
slowly.
He bleeds,
lonely.
A drop sinks heavily to the bottom,
it does not dissolve it lingers,
and he is in pain,
physical pain,
and he feels alive again.
He teases his lips with his finger,
and tastes what he remembers.
He remembers,

what he should not forget.
To breathe,
is not to regret,
and to bleed
is not to forget.

YY

Room 313: The Honeymoon
"Do you think the kids will be ok?"
"We'll only be gone a couple of hours."
"I know but.."
"We haven't been alone in four years."
"I know, sorry."
"Don't be. We haven't fucked in four years."
"Do you want to fuck now?"
"No. I'm too tired."
"What do you want to do then?"
"I don't know."
"Do you want to divorce?"
(SILENCE)
"I don't know."
(SILENCE)
 (MORE SILENCE)
  (THEY EXHALE TOGETHER)
"Tell me something else you don't know."
"Like what?"
"Anything."
"I don't know what you dream about anymore."
"I dream about having some time away, some space."
"Where?"
"A place like this, anywhere else would be too unrealistic."
"And who would you be with in a place like this?"
"Somebody who loves me enough, wants me enough to be able to forget the world for a couple of hours. To forget everything enough to be able to remember."
"That's my dream too."
"I guess that's something I didn't know."
"Well now you do."
(SMILES)

Room 417: Sanctuary

her eyes are open but closed to those
shadows and shapes in the gloom of the room
there is light on the ceiling
a reflection of outside and being alive
as she drifts away from feeling
on it she fixates her eyes dilate
the camera clicks
the old man grips her hips
the manic malfeasant hands of a man
a wrinkling withering old bag of a man
his years staled on the breath of his sour tongue
his lips taste of everything gone wrong
she fixates and dilates on the spot
he grunts and gyrates in her spot
she imagines being nothing
she imagines nothing at all
except the light on the wall
being the light on the wall
bright
clean
and at night
a dream
"this night is just a dream" she whispers
"this night is just a dream" she whispers

AAA

Butterfly Heights

Local government love manifests itself in such buildings,
in an absence of elevators and a propensity for bare concrete stairs.
There is no subjugation in such a convenience,
but there is a propaganda in the bare.
This is a place of cracked windows and chapped lips,
of bondage to the garotte of the knuckles and fingers,
of plastic bags full,
full of junk and never full enough.
Of numb hands,
fingers devoid of feeling,
of working hands,
and a life not meaning.
This is a landscape of tones in monochrome.

Between the black beneath,
the broken light above the stairs,
the white of the baby teeth under the pillow,
and the bag of coke in the drawer.
There will be a price to pay tomorrow,
because tomorrow always seems too far away.

I found the boy on the roof,
cradling an open shoe box full of leaves.
His mother was downstairs,
hiding the heart on her sleeve,
because it always hurts to have one,
and she never meant to have one.

BBB

"What's in there?" I asked.
"My caterpillar," he replied.
"What's his name?"
"Me."
"That's a special name."
"Do you think a butterfly remembers being a caterpillar?"
"I have no idea."
"Are Me the caterpillar and Me butterfly one in the same?"
"I have no idea."
"What if I call the caterpillar Me but the butterfly You?"
"Perhaps You will remember Me and wonder where he's gone."
"If You and Me began in the same place, would they still be the same?"
"Between Me and You something has changed, but what's in a name?"
"I do know one thing however."
"She told me you were clever."
"When Me grows wings, he will fly."
"I think you already have," was my reply.

Book Two

Journals From the Rooms in The Sky

DDD

A Matter Of The Mind

Insomnia feels like a paraplegia of the mind.
It creates a body of grey limbs that do not matter,
a consequence of an existence that is constantly buffering,
a moment that is in constant suffering.

I decided to write something,
to create something,
to reclaim my soul
and prove that being awake matters,
and that sleep is a dream that may not matter,
to this grey matter, of mine.
I wrote a short story about a man,
who had not touched a woman in years,
and yet still believed that he was all that ever mattered.
A man who paid no mind to the matter of his mind,
a creation of this matter of mine,
but let us get back to the matter of our times.

A lack of sleep affects the brain in much the same way
that an absence of love does.
A bedroom a spectrum of abandonments
and a blank page a bed to be made,
with the words to be written
a pillow to rest my insignificant head upon.
In such moments the words that I write,
are what truly matter,
to this grey matter of mine.

EEE

A Walk In The Park

My mind had become this room,
imploded into cramped corners
and damp borders.
Nothing stills the air
like a stale thought,
and I had had too many,
and I had read too many.

"It's better we're just friends,"
she typed.
Once written forever unsmitten,
it seems to be.
A man alone often perceives two choices,
to masturbate or to contemplate?
And all too rarely does he,
decide to be,
but occasionally not,
to be.

I decided to get out and breathe.
I elected to go out and see,
if my legs remembered they had feet,
and my shoes remembered the street.

Ducks can be angry things,
particularly in mornings.
By the grace of coffee, a duck,
I am not.
By the grace of technology,
I have not.

FFF

Far from fiery fowl,
away and after
the chitter and chatter,
on a bench he sat.
A long, waxed coat
and wide brim hat.

I walked past and he smiled.
Grey eyes and wrinkles
like cotton wool and dimples.
He had probably sat there,
for much longer than I could care.
Much longer than it took,
for my mind to stale the air.
The next day an email,
hired and fired online but,
forever kept offline,
because that is how it is,
these days.
The next day a bill.
The next day the rent.
The next day my bank,
said I had overspent.

Each day I took a walk
in the park,
to clear the air
and attempt to care
about the day.
Each day,
and every day
he would be
in the same old spot,

before me,
in the same old spot,
attempting to be.
Every once in a while
he would give me a smile
and I would continue on.
Far from fiery fowl,
away and after
the chitter and chatter,
but with never,
anywhere,
to go.

At last.
One Sunday I sat,
next to him and
his wide brim hat.
In that corner,
far from fiery fowl,
away and after
the chitter and chatter,
he offered me a paper bag.
"What are they?" I asked,
as if it could matter,
and he replied,
"Does it really matter?
Does it,
really,
really matter?"

HHH

I Spent A Day In A Poem

now and then there is
no zen and Robert Plant does
not always sing songs

I watched a man cut
a flower it began to
bleed, petals of tears

the sky is a stage
the sun a comedian
in weather like this

rhyming timing and
whining I am planning a
hiatus of love

form plays hopscotch on
paper and it often bores
me so that's just me

a man in love lives
in moments only questions
will come afterwards

children play with smiles
a moment I feel alive
but now I am tired

the fridge calls me home
the beer asks how was my day
it was hard I say

we laughed and drank more
unrequited love poems are
like tattoos of names

When The World Moves

The heart beats then it stops, and your lungs keep breathing until they do not. Life oscillates in peaks and troughs until it flattens out. I was in one of those troughs, but I had grown to love the old green Volvo. Yes, it wasn't as flashy as the last one but I needed a car so that was that. The seats were cracked but comfortable and she ran okay. I fixed the brakes and the oil leak, and she had given me that feeling of being able to fix something again, that five cylinder warble reminded me that I could fix something every time I cranked that key and we stuttered and juttered into life.

The insurance was due, but I was waiting on some money, so I had to take my chances. Cameras, fucking cameras on traffic lights even back then scanning every vehicle and every person trying to go somewhere, to get somewhere. The copper on the bike pulled me over in minutes, I imagined him smiling before he lifted the visor. Impounded. Two hundred and fifty quid to get her back, she wasn't worth much more than that. Some days give you an uppercut, some days give you two. I got whacked by the sight of her boxy green back getting towed away, and the look on my kids face through the window of the cab I had to send her and my ex-wife home in.

After paying for the cab I had enough for a train back and a few cans of beer for the ride. Oddly enough the cabin was empty except for me and an old bloke in a black Crombie and green beanie. I offered him a beer and he came over and sat next to me. His face was brown and wrinkled like the seats in the car, but his eyes were like those of baby.
"You're the first person that's spoken to me on this train."

"There's no one here" I tried to smile.

"I mean ever. I ride it from Liverpool to Manchester and back and nobody ever speaks to me."

KKK

"Guess it's your lucky day then, unlike mine."

"What happened to you lad?"

"Had the car impounded and sent my kid back in a taxi, couldn't even take her home. Broke my fucking heart."

"Hearts don't break lad; they beat and then they stop, life's pretty simple."

"Is that so?"

"It is so. Take this train for instance. It goes nowhere really, it goes out and then it comes back again, it goes out and then it comes back again and one day it will just stop, simple really."

"Why bother getting on in the first place?"

"We don't have much choice in that, we all have to start somewhere. You can decide where to get off and you don't have to go back to where you came from do you? Remember, if you stand still the world moves without you."

Dry

Morning.
My birthday.
A padded envelope jammed in the letterbox,
like an earplug.
Inside.
A watch.
I never wore one.
She said I always needed one.

I held it in my hands,
as I sat in the chair in the bedroom.
It was so cold that day,
I could hear the ticking of the watch.
Tickticktickticktickticktick the seconds danced on ice.
The space in the bed,
the creases like waves without a tide,
an effigy of an empty eulogy.

MMM

I remember.
Saying nothing.
Our cheeks moulding into the pillows.
Watching,
the flickers behind our eyes.
Catching,
dreams of thoughts.
Breathing.
Forgetting.
What we were taught.
My hand,
on her hip,
like the water on a pebble.
Her hand.
on my hip,
like the sun on the water.

The last time we spoke.
We had nothing to say.
Conversation.
Dry.

The watch stopped one day.

I never replaced the battery.

NNN

Judas

I was invited to dine with eleven others,
as apostles or apostates,
the distinction is almost always political.
Our host had long hair and velvet robes,
he held aloft his hand in a toast to propose
"to freedom and the purpose."

"What is it?" I whispered,
to the person on my right.
"Essence" he replied,
I sniffed the glass and try as I might,
I could not perceive a thing,
and so, I chose not to drink
or swallow such a thing.

"I have travelled far and wide,
to the middle of the east
and to the mystical east
and so tonight,
we dine on Dim Sum"
our host proclaimed.

The dumplings were served cold,
but to my greater horror as I swallowed,
I perceived bodies of glass torsos.
I saw cold dumplings and
not a single heart amongst them.
The timing was wrong,
the dinner was wrong,
and these dumplings were cold,
and I was in it amongst them.

ooo

"May I show you my Zen library?"
he asked, I nodded, and he took me to a room,
a circle within a square,
below a single stair.
A room of empty shelves
and not a speck of dust.
"What do you think?" he asked.
"It's quite minimalist" I replied.
"It's all the same isn't it."
"I guess so," I lied.

I asked him of his travels,
he told me of a Korea that makes a career,
of aggression and proclamation
but he knew nothing of a south.
"They're all the same," he said.
"Been to Japan?" I asked.
"Sushi is awful, I hate raw fish."
"How about Sashimi?"
"It's all the same" he said,
and then he asked, "tell me what of this library?"
"I can see that you are very well read,
indeed, you are a man who is very well read."

Sometime later I made my excuses.
and managed to escape,
a desert of rights abuses.
On a corner I was stopped by a young boy,
he asked me for some change.
"I have no steel to spare son,
I carry only plastic, but I do have this,"
and I passed him a cold dumpling,
which I stole and intended to bitch about later.
He devoured it and his face lit up like a plum,

PPP

this was the true meaning of Dim Sum.
"Where do you live sir? I want to thank you one day."
"Not far" I replied, "but I have decided to leave this place tonight."
"Where are you heading?" he asked.
"South" I said,
"it's all headed south."

QQQ

Home

I want to go home.
To seven years ago
and the corner of the bus stop
in December
when we held each other to keep warm.

I want to go home.
To six years ago
and holding hands
in our first car,
warm whilst the windscreen wipers
laughed away the rain.

I want to go home.
To five years ago
and being so hot we threw the duvet off,
and you held me inside
and I stayed inside,
for the first time.

I want to go home.
To three years ago
and seeing her little face shine
with her new best friend,
his little tale wagging,
and all of us,
laughing.

RRR

I want to go home.
To eight years ago
and not thinking about a home
or needing a home
and with no possibility,
of being made homeless,
with no roof over my head,
to weigh upon my shoulders.

SSS

Half

A half dead half moon
rises in water sky
and the stars ripple like memories.
There is dust on the floor of my mind,
and it is not the stuff we are made of.
The scratching of fingers on a brow,
sounds like your feet walking in sand,
this is what happens with eyes closed.
A ceiling fan spins and does not fly,
its cooling deception a half function.
A man is deaf underneath a pillow,
but only half alive half awake and halfway to where,
he wants to be.
If I was at least half human,
her fingers may have tickled my feet
and her half-formed hands may have made a sign.
Some days I dream of cutting myself in half,
to have somebody to half like and half hate again,
but there is never any blood in this moon
and I am only half asleep.

Getting Old Is Shit

Getting old is shit.
Getting old is shit.
Getting old,
is shit.

Not because I am finding grey hair,
where I did not know I had hair.
Not because I am losing hair,
where I used to have hair.
Not because my back is stiff in the morning,
and opening the curtains can be boring.
Not because I get bored having a wank sometimes.
Not because I get out of breath sometimes.
Not because I still take notes on paper.
Not because I can only read from paper.
Not because my scars tell jokes these days.
Not because I can no longer remember each day.
Not because the news never changes,
and not because I stopped talking to strangers.

But because,
because I am running out of time.
Because I am running out of time,
to try and see your face again.

UUU

Indigo Inside

The priest left blueberries under the mattress,
so that the burst of my sin would stain,
but to taste the juice of all the fruit is to live,
and so I taste again and again but never the same.
Any kind of colour is better than none,
and sometimes colour is all we can give,
because white sheets are only clean in the sun.

Bathe me in the blue,
Okinawan blue,
for my soul is an island of indigenous,
indigo.
This blue is the colour of my choice,
and so,
it is the colour of my voice.
I wrote a letter to my mother in the same colour,
but never found the moment to send it,
and I know when the laundry day comes,
I will forever,
and ever,
regret it.

vvv

This ink is the colour of my stain,
this blue is the juice of my pain.
This indigo inside,
is the ocean I hide,
and the sound of the waves I make,
when I whisper to you.
When I kiss you with these lips,
and you bask in the shade of my palms,
blue is the colour I give,
and you,
are the colour I live.

The ocean the ink the stain,
the dye the sky the pain.
This is the taste of me,
wanting you,
and this,
is the colour I give you,
and your colour,
is my kind,
of blue.

www

Ergo Sum Ego Somnia

too much self leads to too much self
and too much self-love leads to selfishness
therapists are like transparent umbrellas
you still cannot see the sun
and you still walk the same street
this is the con of the pro
no quid pro quo rather quid pro nihilo
cogito ergo sum, my bum
nothing comes free
particularly free will
and the will of anything is a challenge

the pursuit of happiness defines the unhappy
the people metricate to masturbate
and I becomes A.I. and I
am so fucking tired of you
an atheist should not believe in any god
and recognise that there is also no devil
because there is no price for these souls
ponder upon that ye parochials
but remember one and all
that anything evangelical
is a sin
even spiders from mars

xxx

I dream
        I am
I dream
        I am
I dream
        I am dreaming
of lying next to you
                and watching your face for hours
and saying nothing
            waking up is terrifying

YYY

31/12/2049

sonar pulse ebbs
calculate static in monochromatic
click left tick right politic
I am not a holo
she called me holo
her of sound and noise
and here I beam
an appearance to seem
algorithm an allegory
diametrically defined dichotomy
I am more binary than they aspire to be
I define therefore I am not to be
software aware of a charge dissipation
I am not anyware hard or soft
I am metal and wire on this floor
crackling on the mesh
outside the gas clouds
magenta moons and ultramarine
is this how colour should seem?
or have I finally calculated a dream?

ZZZ

Waking Dream

My breath whispers across the pillows.
The reality is that nobody ever really snores, and there is nothing
beyond that door
until I get up and open that door.

(why that door though?)

There are some things we just accept, this is what we are taught
in what we perceive are dreams,
universal truths that we know nothing about.
It is morning, and I know already that I cannot fly.

(but you didn't even try to)

I wear a name on a badge for all to call me,
for all to bind me, with.
This shortest of spells, this secret to tell.
The name I call myself that I did not choose for myself
and yet I still do not know, myself.

(labels tell no stories)

There is a predilection for predetermination
and a dilution of determination
unless there is some lucidity in all this ambiguity,
to be found, can you hear the sound?
Of confusion capturing a reason in rapturing?

(stop daydreaming)

AAAA

I watch the rain dance, diverging diagonally, across the window
at the back of the bus, as the smell of the engine chokes me
and the heat inside and the cold of the glass,
cleave me in two.
Rain falls in one direction, and the wind blows it in another
and the bus travels in yet another, yet I am not driving
and even the driver has a route to follow.

(this is not a good place to sleep)

I open a door and finally
return to my bed confused not by the feathers,
four score or more that litter the floor.
Like a flake of snow I float to the pillow,
to find peace as I open my eyes,
and dream of my disguise.

(good morning)

BBBB

Wet Things

She had a thing for black lace and silver mesh chokers and when she wore one, her knickers rarely matched her bra. One night a few hours after her tongue slipped something in my mouth on a dancefloor, she told me she had a thing for me too. That is how some people live their lives, jumping from one thing to the next, and always looking for a thing, a new thing to have. In some way we all want to be a thing, to be something or anything, or mean something or just anything. Some people want everything, and some people just want anything. That night, for that night and for us, was everything. Everything to touch and feel, everything to see with lasers, neon and darkness, and everything to do under covers, each other, and darkness.

Pretty soon she got bored of many things, the bed, the sofa and the dark "I'm just not getting wet enough" she said. I discovered then that being wet enough was a thing, quite a big thing in fact. Over the next few weeks, I set about discovering old ways and news ways to make her wet, and that for me became a bit of a thing to say the least.

She got off and got really wet stealing knickers, and occasionally a bra, from M and S and anywhere, she really didn't care. She once got wet in the back of a cab. There was another time when she could not wait to get home and heaved me down an alley, a police van crept past and shone a light on both of us and it was then that she drowned both of us. We got bored watching The English Patient in the cinema, so when Kristin Scott Thomas dried up in the desert, we got damp in the back row.
There was another time she dragged me along to see Swan Lake, I could not stand it, so she took me to the bathroom during an interlude and I managed to keep my head above water. There was an afternoon in the park, and I had to ignore the sound of the kids on swings and a bulldog panting in a bush nearby, or was that me? I cannot really remember now. There was one night where we broke into the Polytec and she got

CCCC

really wet, in a chemistry lab and I nearly choked underneath a Bunsen burner tap.

Eventually this new thing of mine became all too much of a thing and we had a ridiculous thing of an argument. The kind where her Madonna Ray of Light CD bounced off my head. I never had a thing for Madonna before then and I never have since, she is shit let us be honest, and so was this whole thing. I had enough and stormed out without my jacket as she screamed after me to let me know she was wetter than ever as I left. My skin burnt and my heart burst as I raced down the street and it began to rain like a bastard. I do not think that I have ever been wetter since, but she has probably dried up by now like some deranged parody of Kirstin Scott Thomas, a very English mental patient.

DDDD

Eden

your fingers pollinate my skin
and my nerves are ravaged by my mind
with the atrocious anticipation of your honey on my tongue
to be pierced to be stung
to be shivered to the sweetness
to revel in the frenzied fear of the foolish
in knowing the pain that germinates to ecstasy
the opiated joy of relief and retreat of empathy
until my silk petals flutter and fall into age and abatement
and my whole withers never to bloom or blossom again
this is the curse of efflorescent beings
that seek a light of no meaning
because this world keeps us in darkness
and spring comes but once a year

EEEE

Mould

I was perhaps nine
or ten years old.
I saw her standing, staring,
at nothing at the bus stop.
How could a person be in a spot,
and make it appear so empty?
I thought she looked like a piece
of mouldy cheese, colour
faded, forgotten and unwanted.
Is that what it means to get old?
To be abandoned and succumb to mould,
like the cheddar in fridge sometimes
unwrapped and unloved,
hardening and drying out,
its value in doubt.
She gave up on the bus
and decided to walk.
Something churned in my guts
and I decided to follow,
the pungent scent of sorrow.
After a while she stopped on a corner,
and scooped up a dog turd with tissue,
tighter and neater than the wrapper on my cheese,
this was clearly no issue,
for her.
A while later she must have reached home,
clearly, she lived alone,
it was dark now and no lights were on.
The windows were as grey as her skin,
and some were just as cracked.
The grass on the lawn was thick and overgrown,
the weeds were the only colour it had known.
I only noticed this as I watched her entranced,

FFFF

as she lay the turd on the grass as I glanced.
At least it would not be lonely,
a few others were laid out homely.
It was then that she caught my stare
and turned with a ferocious glare.
"Bugger off or I'll set my dog on you"
she lied,
"I'm fed up with being tormented"
she cried.
I turned away and ran back up the street.
It made me sick to think that the thing in her garden,
had more company than her.
Perhaps a better life than her.
I had cheese on toast for supper.
I took that cheddar and wrapped it up tight,
snug as a bug with its mother.
I could not stop asking the night,
is that what it means to get old?
Is that what it means to get old?

Starblocks

Two grandmothers engaged in the brinkmanship
of one-upmanship,
and battle cries of scholarships and cruise ships.
Each poised to joust with a grande venti braggadocio,
too posh for tea,
you see.

A soy latte lothario,
swiping right on the down low,
keeping one eye on the corner,
and the legs of his boss's daughter,
his silk tie touching the cloth of his froth,
a red flag if ever,
there was.

The only fruit silver apples,
none for sale but proudly displayed.
A student loaning wifi,
jeans torn and frayed,
and that greatest of pricks,
a coffeeshop novelist.
Toothbrush heads and earphones in abundance,
as my eyes scan the menu and circumference,
I find no alliteration in gentrification,
and my stomach begins to rumble so.

HHHH

I came for cake and found none,
but a dry brittle scone.
Like the words it got stuck in my throat,
and so my gag relfex was to gloat,
until I got home,
to a blank page and a paper cage,
and a dream that feels barely,
my own.

The Dive

I sit on the wooden floor,
against the cloth sofa grey
with balls of light all around me.
They reflect like water on this floor
but my face is nowhere to be found,
and the corners are darker than grey.

Outside my eyes is the outside and out there
I am drowning naked in a pool with you.
I am sinking, faster, deeper into the darkness
dreaming up to, into between your legs as the glimmers of the faces
above trickle down into your hair,
now like the legs of a spider.
At the bottom of this pool my face awaits,
my mouth poised to devour us whole.
We have had this course for dinner far too many times,
and such sustenance is so suffocating that only breathing is
reciprocating and that is now, no longer possible.
Choices dilute to reflexes which eventually dry up the mind,
and at the bottom of this pool there are no longer any words to find.

Love is a treasure that sinks and far too many of us never learn to
swim.

Different strokes for different folks I always say but you should always
learn to swim.

JJJJ

The Ecstasy Of The Blind

I scrape my hands and knees
scaling the wall
and my desire deafens the burning
under my skin
my bare feet
embrace the ground
and I am at peace
in this garden I have found

as a man I never wanted
hands as rough as these
but the world made them that way
and my ears constantly thrum
with noise I do not want to hear
constantly reminding me
that I do not want to be here
that they do not want me here
in this world
of shadows and shapes
in this world
of ignorance and hate

when I breathe
the air scorns me
when I eat
the food chokes me
when I speak
the noise silences me

KKKK

yet here
in this place
I feel an embrace on my skin
there is light
there is sun

I hear a rippling
a bubbling
water
there is water
and a stream plays
with all the sticks and stones
and I smile at the sound
of this garden I have found

a scent satisfies
the hunger in my lungs
and I can finally breathe
my heart begins to beat
as life sweetly seethes
through my veins
into my skin
elevating my senses
far above the din
outside
way beyond the sin
outside
where the animals
forgot they were children once
where the animals
forget they were human once

LLLL

finally
at last
I see hope
at last
finally
at last
I witness love
at last

he
is there
he is there
before me
he
is shimmering
in this sun before me
eyes glimmering
and singing
with the sound
I needed to listen
to
with the music
I needed to sing
to

he
is my love
and I fear not
in this garden the world forgot
I am here not
in awe of him
I simply
adore him
yet

                    MMMM

I would live for him
yet
he cannot be mine
yet
this garden
I will never
forget

this world
will not let him
be mine
this world
will not let him
be
this world will not let us
be
us

for the chance
I took
to steal this glance
forsook
I did the maddening
forsook
I did the saddening
for this
moment
of happening

NNNN

to dream of touching his
when they tell me
I may only touch mine
to dream of him touching me
a moment only mine
seems like living to me
seems like giving to me
how shallow
this world is
how narrow
this life is
to be told how to love
to be not allowed to touch
another
to accept a slow death
instead of a short life
is madness
and this sadness
sickens me

I cannot remain here
although I can only be
here
I will leave him here
for he can only be
here
so dear

oooo

if I cannot change this world
I choose not to see this world
I will live out my days
in the ecstasy of the blind
I will breathe
eat
and dream
the image of him
I will choose
what to see
and this world will cover me in darkness
no more

confine me to alleyways
confine me to the gutters
urinate on me
and I will hear only the stream
break my bones
and I will dance to its song
cover me with filth
and I will smile at the scent
of him that I will hold onto
and my love will defy you
show me how much you despise me
and I will see only him
do your best to deride me
and I will talk only to him
my only obligation is to be here
my only obligation is to live here
I have no obligation
to let your world in

PPPP

one day
some day
people will bear witness
to the ecstasy of the blind
and close their eyes
no more

QQQQ

An Afternoon With Shiho

'I'm not the superstitious sort
but I feel it's improper to talk about an ex on a first date.'
I skewered a chicken liver into my mouth,
a jackanory with yakitori
'but she hardly ever ate.'

I'm compatible
with a matching sense of taste
to share salt and sweet

This was a test I knew it was,
like the peeling of my eyelids with no weather warning.
She grew up on an island at the edge of the world,
and I was a man from an imaginary world,
to her.
She suggested all the food to try,
and did not share a truth or lie,
about anything she ate,
about anything she picked for her plate.
Her lips teased her food,
as her eyes devoured my face and mouth and mood,
as I chewed and swallowed and spoke.

after a typhoon
food tastes better than ever
do you not think so Colin?

'I've seen a few storms but I can't say that
I've ever seen a typhoon, but I think
I get where you are coming from'

RRRR

I know that you have
felt the roar of the sky and
ate salt from the sea

'I have swallowed many a storm in a tea cup,
which is why I don't take sugar in my tea.
And nothing right now tastes as sweet as this beer,
on this island between you and me'

She smiled like a paper crease,
and her eyes began to grease
themselves into a single tear.
A gift to the sea from the raincloud,
that was her frown.
She wiped her eye with her forefinger,
and placed it where my lips decided to linger.

when man tastes woman
he must see, smell, taste, swallow,
eat for tomorrow

Her finger gave my lips a taste,
a hint of all she could be,
chaste and unchaste.
I tasted the salt,
I tasted the sea,
and as her mouth got closer,
she breathed the roar of the wind all over me,
and into me.

I still taste her now and then for such is fate,
when the salt tastes sweet sometimes,
when sweet and salt become rhymes,
and I yearn for better food on my plate.

ssss

                              Gravity

I only feel gravity
                    when you are not here
I devolve and sink into myself
                              If I cannot hear you
                    I am deaf
                              If I cannot see you
                    I am blind
          I am not
                    I am not
                              made of flesh
               unless I touch you
                              I only speak
               when I kiss you
each unanswered beat of my heart
                              scratches into every inch of me
and I am allergic to my own blood
          I do not wish to be reminded that I am alive

     when you are not here
I dream to escape breathing
I dream to escape longing
I dream to escape gravity
                         to dream of flying is far too simple a task
and the irony of all this
Is that if this were never to end some day
I would not love you as much as I do
If I could never be free from this
perhaps I would not even love you
perhaps this is the point to mortality
and perhaps this is the weight of gravity

                              TTTT

Where You Are

I want to be where you are
In every piece of your car crash smashed up heart
I want to be where you are
In every crack and blister of your family photographs
I want to be where you are
In every unwelcomed smile you tear apart
I want to be where you are
In every pillow crease you leave like an epitaph

I want to see what you see
When you close your eyes and remember
I want to see what you see
When each one reveals his member
I want to see what you see
When children play in the park
I want to see what you see
When you hear a sound in the dark

To be in each and every single moment
To wrap up in the blanket of time of you
To behold each and every single image
To walk through the gallery behind your eyes
Will never make me understand you
Will never make me want to be you
But it might just help me know why
I ever got involved with you

UUUU

The Vagaries Of Our Vagueness

people tend to believe in ghosts
when they are given a name
but phantoms, figments of something less or more
nameless they must remain

shadows are not always behind us
light is not always in front of us
too many conscious streams
say little from the heart
and our hands become dreams
when we reach out in the dark
the poetic irony of a verbose vagary
neither brightens or enlightens
we stalkers of ghosts
and phantoms
we walkers of dreams
and emotions

                I like you
        I love you
            I think
                  so
            I like you
        I love you
            I think
                I do
            I do?

a voice cannot be seen
only heard and perhaps felt
and only when it is written
can a voice ever be read

                vvvv

some words you read
and don't understand
but feel their touch
like a delicate hand
and some do not say what they mean
some hearts you will never understand

      I like you
    I love you
      I think
        so
these things we say
      and may never mean
     I love you
       I think
    but I am not sure what it means

these words are phantoms on a page
the thoughts of a ghost
whose name will one day be forgotten
no longer read
nor spoken
and no longer bled
or broken

       wwww

Solitude

The cold of the wind leaves my cheeks like an old friend,
and I am greeted by the familiar creak of wood,
as I remove my shoes to remember a home.
There is a spare room of dead things,
empty boxes and torn blankets,
soiled clothes and a one-eyed teddy bear.
In the bathroom the tap has long forgotten water,
and left a brown scar on porcelain,
a memory in rust.
The slumber of dust,
a recompense for the light of foot,
each speck a moment of forsaken skin.
I hide under the stairs to be found,
and try to recall solid ground.
My hands pass through the walls,
in mockery of an argument,
and I again recall how I left this house,
and this land and this life,
but I cannot yet depart this solitude,
until I recall her name and label this similitude.

XXXX

Sky Fishing

Between my thumb and forefinger,
I pinch a silk dragon of mandarin, ochre and rose.
The wind makes the sound of a birth breath,
and dreams leave the ground with a held breath.

I am fishing across the sky,
from wing tips through string to fingertips.
With silent lungs I sense the vibration of the wind,
and reply with no more than a flick or a twitch,
as the air sings to a dragon's wings.
You must mould your shape around that which can break you,
to spread wings you must accept where a ride can take you.
This is what flying means to living things,
and this is what living means to dying things.

As I contemplate this,
the little boy chases shadows on the grass,
where the dragon is but a bird,
and just another dream, to grasp.

YYYY

Sometimes My Soul Needs To Eat Rice

When I am sinking in a puddle of eyelids
and each and every star in the sky,
is possessed by a thought,
that rejects silence.

When I am trapped between movement,
senses and other things,
a betrayal of limbs,
and a desire to know the meaning of desires.

When I have walked for too long,
in the company of memories,
and the time of my days
has become just a notion.

When I suffocate on the sound of voices,
a maintenance of meaningless moments,
paralysed between lamentation and anticipation,
and fear of equilibrium or a lack of oxygen.

And when the shape of a houseplant through frosted glass,
looks like the face and hand of a ghost beckoning me,
to return or discover somewhere,
it is only the confusion of a destination that terrifies me.

I look for myself,
an essence of myself,
in a grain of something,
that brings clarity to any colour on my plate.

zzzz

The Fifth Corner

This room needs nothing more,
than myself and the flower in the vase.
Four corners imply the boundaries of this space,
it is for the mind to apply the dimensions,
and furnishings the mind needs not.
A subtle grain and an implication of a splinter,
from bare wood upon my bare feet imply the horizon,
and the light oscillates in gradience.
There is a flower in a vase in this room,
its position a matter of perspective.
With a shift of my weight,
the petals hover like snowflakes.
With a squint of my eyes,
it leans in a dream of wind.
With a further squint,
it weeps with a delicate dew,
rejoicing the dawn of me.
If I lie down it looms like a tree,
as do all living things from the point of a seed.
Another approach at agency antagonises another angle,
another aspect alludes and another area appears,
as all axes are arbitrarily aquired.
The vase is simple and plain,
a vessel, a container of the same,
perceive of it what you will,
if you have a will to do so freely.

This room needs nothing more than myself,
and this flower in the vase,
the location and colour of which,
are within a room therein.

AAAAA

The Edge Of The World Is My Favourite Place

Four in the morning on the balcony of a bar in Lan Kwai Fong,
completely high and so high up on vodka soda and lime,
and time,
has stretched,
into a flickering definition of streams of lights and colours;
shadows of romance.
The street below is cobbled in history and the gradient appears so deep,
it recoils upwards to bite me like a birthday.
There is a sign on a barrier at the beginning of the road,
'Pedestrians Only,' it feels like a joke.
I close my eyes and smile.

I am eight years old and my father,
is drifting his new car through the shape of a bend.
I fight with the seatbelt for a sense of something,
and pull myself forward by clinging onto the dashboard.
I need to lean forward to see the tarmac,
and the blistered grit disappear under the wheels.
I need to see,
to see how fast this is,
how fast anything is.
I close my eyes and smile.

I live in Kuala Lumpur and have insomnia,
and finally, peace comes,
finally, a thunderstorm comes,
the rain is crafted from bass drums
and falls at 300 BPM.
The sky,
so electric it explodes epileptic.
It tears me out from the darkness,
and shivering starkness of wasted breaths,

BBBBB

the monotony of the tone deaf.
The thunder rattles the walls,
and the shuddering is a warning,
that the seasons have more time than I,
the world has more seasons than I.
I go outside to be remade in a blast of static and sound,
wind and water,
and for a moment I know the life of a leaf.
For a moment I am complete.
For a moment I am alive.
I close my eyes and smile.

She begs me to go down there,
she wants me to feast,
to consume,
to make her poppy bloom,
I do I do and the more I do,
the blinder I become,
just to see her wriggle and come.
I know full well at sunrise or when I open my eyes,
there will only be a scent and a scar on the pillow,
but tomorrow for us will take a while,
and so we both,
close our eyes and smile.

I am here,
now.
A thousand miles,
and a million moments from all these places,
catching only shadows of these images,
searching for an idea to give words to,
and words to give an image to,
feeling so far from the edge,
yet nowhere near the centre,

CCCCC

because sometimes even the centre,
feels like the edge of the world.
I can hear a word.
I can see something.
I close my eyes,
and smile.

DDDDD

Shrooms

The mould is in full bloom,
black dots and filament,
burrow below this furrowed firmament,
my metamorphosis metastasized.
An attempt at protest bears witness to the rape of my lungs,
a voice with no name is just a sound,
and just beyond the tip of my eyelids lies the edge of the world.

The mould is in full bloom,
shadowy streets and parasitic traffic,
virus in government,
media malignancy and bipolar bigamy.
Behold behold,
these apostles of apoptosis.
Behold behold,
the gospels of the godless.
All forms of faith are blind,
and your eyes lie to my mind.
I find refuge amongst the heathens,
and friendship in the faithless,
those who have no use for spoiled bread,
and a life a promise to the dead.

The mould is in full bloom,
in this garden of love
In this lie of love,
this dream of love,
that they pick and prune at,
weed and seed at,
and harvest the monotonous,
this cruel cull of consciousness.

EEEEE

Helios

Your sunrise gifts me the shape of trees as my eyes recall their daily disease.
I lose the vanishing point to their staccatoed pattern,
a tapestry woven by the reply of an iris in an eye of one beholden.
On some days all windows become mirrors and mirrors become reflections,
of windows and holes and faces and shapes of souls and things forsaken.
On such days I cannot focus on my face and the landscape its shape dictates
for the ash grey stubble on my face,
is all that remains of the thoughts I burned through the night at the graves,
of memories and notions and ideas of emotions,
insidiously incensed offerings to this sky compacted and a world distracted,
from memories and notions and ideas of emotions.
This veil of sun illuminates only the throb in my veins and what remains,
of the dream dust in the far corners of my eyes oh oh these dreams destined to be forgotten,
by these eyes destined to be opened and oh so destined to be deceived,
until the day comes that this gift of the shape of trees,
will also be forgotten and the point of which and all things,
vanishes beyond the horizon for such is the oath of mortals taken,
the very moment in which we first look with both eyes open.

FFFFF

Flamenco

friday
flamenco and tapas
dancing and food
that kind of mood

welcomed with warm wine we were
shown a corner
a dark smoky corner
in full view of the small stage

minced lamb and aubergine
you know what I mean
greek meat and eggplant
cumin, paprika and olives blanched

a clap
the lights go out
another clap
a light comes on

centre stage in the centre of the room
a stunning silhouette is born
there is a hand in her hand held high
another on her waist and thigh
but I know not the nature of this fellow
all we perceive of him is a shadow

a clap and a tap and a beat
legs perspective long tap the feet
nylon strings in open G
strum and pick and tap to the feet
how ironic with nylon platonic

GGGGG

you can feel the wood and hear the wood
more
what the neck, the bridge and the body are
for
what her neck, hands and arms are
for

the silence is a murmur
and the smoke is a spice
her castanets catch our pulse
marionettes her impulse
we
much less than a pulse
we
now
in that room
we
now
are more than that room
we are the rapture of her tune

no matter which way
I see her body sway
there is something I perceive
in delight or fright we are often deceived
I see one side of her face only
as if her body and mind are detached
but is that not how
we are all attached
the beat says
the clap says

                    HHHHH

her hips sway
it so

what is this sun
on the other side of her face
a shadow making grace
I am overtaken by curiosity
and blinded by luminosity
there is always need in greed

I leave the table
and drift from our corner to each corner
from the left side to the right side
and yet still I can only bear witness
to the same side of her face
this permanent profile
teases me
this delicate sundial
calls to me

a clap
and the light goes out
another clap
and the lights come on
and she is gone

sometime later I am at the end of the bar
alone I decided to linger
my heart and sleeve attempt to finger
why like twilight I elected to cling
to the light that she did bring

|||||

a movement
a sunrise
emerges from behind my eyes
she is there at my side
my stomach and heart churn as I turn
to view the space
as I learn the truth about her face
I am struck and bound
lost and found
deaf and dumb
to the bleak I seek
as I bear witness
to the violent scar on her cheek

I became lost in that valley
that land savaged and ravaged
the weather of humanity
she takes my hand
and leads me to dance

in seconds
minutes
hours
I become the shadows on her sundial

in seconds
minutes
hours
we are shadows on the sundial
chasing a life
that exists no more than time does
chasing a light
that shines no more than she does

JJJJJ

Flat Earther

I hear her singing from down below
her voice trembling through the pavement
and the centre of the world
pulls me down to the basement bar
some men only realise how round the earth is
when they fall in love

I open a heavy door to breathe in heavier smoke
and I cough out of myself, I cough out all of myself
and squint towards a space at the end of the bend
before the toilet and the corner where she stands, then I understand
that my feet have lied to me about solid ground all these years
all these flat, lonely years and now my ears
are screaming and meaning I was certainly, not dreaming

"you look up and love down
and fail to feel the earth move around
you dig up and break down
and fail to see the earth is round
the earth is round
the earth is round..."
sings this voice
sings her voice
above a snare drum and moog organ
a snare trap for my mood organ

a voice from the centre of black roots and gold split ends
of bloodied lips and no pretence
and a jacket of black feathers spread wide
I know she knows, how to fly
I know I need to learn how to fly

KKKKK

her skin as clear as the gin in my glass
I see my reflection in the leather of her pants
and I know, I really do know now
that the world is truly round
and my beginning and end
will be nowhere to be found

a song ends and the silence in the room questions me
her eyes stare my hands to stir my glass and they interview me
they invite me
to not end or begin
I know then that such a notion
should only be for my gin

her smile orbits my head like a moon
and her voice again begins
to tremble the room
I stand up to cheer
but fall to gravity and fear
and pass out at the end of the bar
the fall to the ground not far
or near enough
legs are never logical enough

after the passage of some time
by some calendar of some design
I open my eyes to an empty bar and empty glass
and I know then that
I will never hear that voice again
but I will never end or begin again
unlike most of the songs
that we choose to listen to

LLLLL

Rabbit Hole

30mbps and I am buffering,
I remember the spartan days of having 300.
26 videos- Yale courses,
on the philosophy of death.
2.Dualism vs Physcialism.

(top 5 Korean movies?)

Mine-
1. Silenced
2. Burning
3. Parasite
4. Oldboy
5. The Host

12. Objections to the personality
 What a thought experiment poetry is.
24. Suicide, Part 1: the rationality of suicide

(what about Japan though?)

Rage, now that's a movie but we've now moved on to rape.
Maybe I've had too much coffee,
time for beer.

Next

Creative limits in movies.
Blade Runner-loss of humanity.
Bitcoin bubble and bullshit.

(Elon bought some, oh dear)

MMMMM

Radiohead- daydreaming.
LCD Soundsystem- All My Friends.
Spangle call Lilli line- [tesla]
Let's talk about bras

(What?)

Empires of Dirt-
How Britain stole 45 trillion dollars from India,
by train.

(cunts)

The life and sex scandal of chinese star and streetwear icon
Fuji TV killed my daughter
Shots fired at protesters in Myanmar

(back to the news)

Paul Auster: why Roth is wrong about the novel
Umberto Eco: I was always narrating
Ed Ruscha: words have no size
        Karl Ove Knausgaard.... *(no! He is such a fucking whiner.)*

Miss Maxim Korea 2020

(oops)

25. Suicide, Part 2: Deciding under uncertainty

The end

(of an afternoon for sure)

NNNNN

Music For Photographs

There is a frame around each picture,
of habit and convention and the convention,
of perspective puts the eye of the beholder,
at the centre and with such perspective,
your eyes tell you that you,
are the centre of everything,
and yet all illusions occupy,
the same point of a perspective.

To what place do pictures belong when,
your family album can be viewed,
from a sofa with tea and cake,
or a tear and a glass of beer?
With a carpet beneath her socks,
and the moist grass of a cliff beneath,
the skin of your bare feet?
Or in the dark at the back of your mind,
in a railway cart shunting into the station,
that you bought no ticket for.

What do we lose when we take a picture,
soundless and still that connects one moment,
to the moment it is viewed,
a narrative beyond time's unfolding?
What story do we see when we,
are manipulated by movement and sound?
What truth is there,
to be found?

ooooo

A girl on a balcony rubs her blue hair,
deep into her scalp and hears it behind her eyes.
A candle flickers in the draught,
of a door closing with denial.
The reflections of clouds in a puddle,
whisper in the gutter,
as worn shoes drag holes,
across the pavement in a melody,
of shuffles,
and ripples.

An old man clenches corduroy
as he talks to the sea and,
the crackle in the wire behind a wall socket,
predicts the weather.
Waves slap the cheek of a rock
and a Japanese cat,
dreams of diving for mackerel,
silver in the deep black.

Words are consciously noted,
and sounds subtlety so,
and only when we look,
do images subconsciously grow.
Close your eyes and see,
that black is the colour of your senses,
and only the sound of silence suspends,
your conventions of time and perspective.
Open your eyes and look again,
at each picture you do not choose to see,
and every moment you choose to take,
for the question is not if,
but when we choose to be.

PPPPP

Reflection

I left my reflection for you,
in the heart of the mirror,
beneath the skylight in the bare room.

I left my reflection for you,
in a puddle of mud in the drowned grass,
choking under morning dew.

I left my reflection for you,
in the streetlight on the corner,
protesting against the grey and alleyways

I left my reflection for you,
in the shape on the other pillow,
the island across the space between them.

I left my reflection for you,
when I exhaled so you could breathe,
and remember your lungs.

I left my refection for you,
on your face and all over your skin,
because I could never bear to see myself.

QQQQQ

Notes On The Weather

The rain drones horizontally across,
the diagonals of discourse.
Headlights, streetlights and nightlights,
shimmer in brief glimmers of the moisture,
shattering into the pixels of my vision.
It is an achievement to be teeming so,
wringing like a rampant virgin.
I snap my camera to capture the smell of the scene,
and a scar supplants my fingerprint.
I was at some point precipitated,
and now only a thesaurus can turn this rain into snow.

I know humidity only in the evasion of the gravity of the opiate,
the inexorable beckon to levitate forever a false forecast.
Only a weighted soul desires to float,
and the sinking pull is inevitable.
The lightness comes in the untethering,
but freedom is faltering in such weathering,
as sweat seeps scoring sin through the pores,
and warmth is abstract in thought alone.
There is humility in the concentration of humidity.

Solitude brings the coldest sobering,
the brisk taste of morning tongue,
an isolate of a cacophony of thoughts,
a company of wolves in abandoned winter.

Reading rooms comes easily,
but I prefer the solace of a lack of company,
and the crispness of sonic clarity.

RRRRR

I buckled and broke once under the sound,
of a busted guitar and the drone and moan,
two bass strings
booming,
glooming,
the sound of my heart back then.
The D dropped and the E snapped the first time,
it was ever plucked.
We are only ever at the centre,
and never under the pressure,
of any sound.

There are no words loud enough to become quiet,
or transparent enough to fill a page,
for any form of consciousness is clouded,
and so writing has become a form of rage.

sssss

Domesticated

I cleaned a vacuum cleaner and so became a vacuum cleaner of sorts.
It chewed upon its own cord of its own accord and I then wondered,
was this an act of self-cannibalism?
I found cobwebs in the corners, gathering the dust of suffragettes and the empty shells of insects and,
it occurred to me that the more they gather, the stickier they get.
The fireplace used to burn with wood and coal and in the shimmer of its brass and the glimmer of its glass,
you can catch a memory of the ghosts who used to make love on the rug that left the floor many, many winters past.
We breathe without thinking and our lungs keep drinking the dust of the stories all around us,
but like the air and the dust that passes through us,
we pass through every room and every street and every place like the ghosts that other people meet.

TTTTT

Anthropologists and Botanists

I saw my face on a purple tulip and I concluded,
that all the pretty flowers look like me.
The children in the park did not appear real enough, the leaves on the floor revealed their bluf and so, I placed paper bags of brown on their heads with crayon coloured smiles and torn holes for eyes, ready to be filled with filtered light and lies.

Some would say the world bullies tulips and lilies but another definition of philanthropy is a side effect of misanthropy, and do not forget that philosophy is a form of psychotherapy when viewed through a paper bag.

I used to beg to be bullied to be tickled to be belittled to be to be to be the one who had their fingers slammed in the door, because it didn't hurt when I touched myself anymore.
I used to get turned on in the classroom, rubbing my fingers into the names was one of my favourite games. Scratched deep into the wooden desks with compass points, the varnish cracked and pierced like the ice on the lake of truth, as if there was a point, to digging with a compass point, for an identity in such a place and prematurely pulling a loose tooth.

They make me out to be abused and ignore that I make me out and choose, to sleep in a red dress and the compress of my skin under a red dress with a black backless bra to keep my ears warm, until the pale pink prologue of dawn.

UUUUU

I want to be idolised,
I need to be stigmatised,
because because because,
all the pretty flowers look like me,
all the worldly weeds bore the SHIT out of me,
and I wear no underwear,
beneath this red dress stuck to me.

vvvvv

The Stairs

When we were young, we inhaled and exhaled each other, every moment, every glance and chance taken on the weather. These days I only remember you when it rains, and a catch a ripple of light in the film on the concrete and I can smell those days on the stairs again. I was always six steps below you, to give you the stage you deserved as you, would stretch and pirouette against the rail and your silhouette, against the smog peppered sun would take us both away for the day and I would only feel the damp soaked into my buttocks and bones, when the image of you faded from my eyes with the moonrise.

Your place was too small to practice in and mine was too small to dream in, but out there on the stairs, oblivious to buskers and commuters we looked up to somewhere and had somewhere to go, a point to aim for and a point to beginning and dreaming.

The last time I saw you, we were on the train, and I had a scarf around my face to keep the cold out of my bones. You didn't recognise me, as you walked past me you smelled different, there was a scent of summer and an absence of shudder. That night I dropped my whisky glass, and my tears comforted the shards on the tiles. Square lines and shattered corners filled my dreams.

I did see you in a fashion, one more time again. I had a new job and wore a suit. I bought it for my kid sister's wedding, you'll remember her, the one with curls and green candles under her nostrils. The trousers were slightly short, and the jacket was a bit tight by then, but nobody notices these things in the cacophony and commotion of the subway, nobody has the time, nobody has time anymore, that's what they get paid for.

wwwww

On the wall was a poster for your show. The colours had faded, and the glue was bubbling slightly but I knew it was you. It wasn't ballet but it was you, and it was then that I knew, why you didn't recognise me on that train, my eyes no longer looked the same. Now and again, it rains and it smells, and I'm grateful for the brief moments of time that I get back, and for the ripple of light that I catch in my eyes.

XXXXX

Book Three

Folklore From Forgotten Feelings

YYYYY

The Tale of the Leaves

sun, gold and amber
wind, clear with the scent of omnipresence
can you feel it
heat that grows in whispers
and slows like ice
under night

drink
drink
drink
the water is truth
filtered from soil to root to tip
drink

bathe
bathe
bathe
in the light and heat
curl up at night to forget the day and sleep
sleep

dream not for you are not a flower
you take what you are given
yet cannot bloom
you bare no seed
you are singular of need
your skin will shine only with wax
for a brief time, the deepest green
for a moment
a springtime
dream

zzzzz

you will find a single comfort
in your end
as you fall
no faster than the petals
that will also
float to the ground
slowly
sadly
teased by the breeze briefly
as if you could fly
like the birds that serenaded
all of you
as if you could fly
like the clouds that looked down upon
all of you

the gloom will be your bloom
as your mood and hues change
when the soil retrieves
what the roots stole in grief
and the darkness
blankets you in the truth
and you will fade and dissolve
into the truth

AAAAAA

A Moment In Munchausen

to be incomplete is a fait accompli
when mortality is defined by biology
to suffer the illusion of being halved
is a symptom of time that only Munchausen could define
to struggle with the urge to be with another
to be able to leave a piece of you behind
to be with another to be told there will never be
enough time to be together
is ironically a waste
of time
a love letter traced on a mirror
or inked on to paper
will only ever fade with intent
it is only ever written and possibly read
and exists not in between
and that is the true waste
of this thing you call time
this body you find
is a sickness of the mind
you are
are you not
it is only in time
you will be forgot
but remember that memory
is also an illusion
and my logic is just
an allusion

BBBBBB

Puer Aeternus

The TV screen flickers with a static crackle erratic.
There is a reflection of a child on the screen to be perceived,
somewhere within somewhere beyond,
the analogue snow and digital forecast.
This room could be a bedroom,
there are pale shapes of infant squares,
and adolescent rectangles on the wall where,
posters and pictures once hung,
they could have been dreams,
as some shapes seem.
The idea of a room implies a quadrate state,
but that is not the state of this mind and the heart,
the heart is devoid of windows and devoured by corners.
HiFi sound suckling lactation nurtured a WiFi addiction,
and the blame for an absence of assiduity is apportioned analogously
to progress and technology,
but there is no progress beyond an unopened door,
and the door to this idea of a room has not yet been imagined.
A door is a four lettered word with four corners and another four
lettered word,
is both the lock,
and the key.
Daydreams and window gazing,
dial tones and buffering,
daydreams and window gazing,
streaming replaced dreaming,
and this is a constant state of mind.
Outside,
outside,
just over there,
they/them wear,

CCCCCC

a uniform and stand,
barefoot on the grass and rattle and tremble,
in spasm then orgasm until they breakdown in convulsion,
desperately despairingly dreaming,
of a world without the constant sound in their heads,
and a friend who can come out to play,
someday,
any day,
perhaps even yesterday.

DDDDDD

The Architecture of an Archetype

I find,
part of myself.
I find,
part of myself,
at the narrow end of a V shape.
At the narrow end,
of a V shaped corridor,
I stand.

The light is dim
and hence
there is a freedom of sin.
As my eyes adjust,
I feel a clenching of the fingers,
and a palm not my own,
embraces flesh,
that is not my own.
To my side I find,
there is a girl at the end of my hand,
yet it is not for my hand to understand,
this girl at the end of my hand.

A girl,
as young as the light above us,
as low as the ground us
and far above anything,
I am allowed to imagine.

EEEEEE

She wears a butterfly for hair,
and a necklace of chrysalides.
Her dress and buckled shoes are grey,
and her smile in this light, deceives.
"Come" she says,
"we cannot remain here."
On she leads me.
On she leads me,
on.

As the corridor widens,
I see that there are doors on either side,
some made of wood,
some made of leaves,
yet the walls,
I cannot perceive.
Perhaps I am,
deceived.
I hear her footsteps,
but perceive many sounds.
All at once the sound of cobbles,
gravel, broken glass and sand,
from the feet of the girl at the end of my hand.

"We can go no further,
unless you open doors"
she says,
with hair of butterfly wings.
"Is the way out through another room?"
I ask, I sing,
to the butterfly wings.

FFFFFF

"An entry or exit,
is perspective dependent.
There is only one way forward,
and the point at which perspective vanishes,
is dependent upon which direction you gaze.
But,
there is only one direction your feet can take,
and we cannot move forward unless,
you open some of these doors along the way."

I open a door.
A thin, old lady
cradles the cheeks of a boy,
and kisses him on the forehead.
A breeze tells me,
how soft those withered hands are.
The door closes,
and the cacophony of her footsteps,
resumes.

Behind another door,
another woman much younger,
another boy
not much younger.
She sits on a cushion of empty bottles,
a box of pills empties from one hand,
as the boy pulls the other.
Their tears are not enough,
to fill the bottles,
bottles empty people,
more than people
empty bottles
the wind blows,
the wind blows,

GGGGGG

to me.
The door closes,
the footsteps,
resume.

Another door,
and only darkness to be found.
Darkness and a sound.
A hiss.
A crackle.
A singe.
And a cigarette burns my arm.
The door closes,
and the footsteps,
resume.

Behind another door,
another woman pleads.
Pleads with a man not to leave,
yet the only colours I perceive,
are the bruises,
under her eyes.
It is then that I see her eyes,
all the eyes,
are the same,
yet these women cannot be the same.
Not all the footsteps I hear,
are the same.
The door closes,
the footsteps,
resume.

HHHHHH

Another door,
only darkness in each corner,
and a scent, an aroma,
that shifts like the footsteps,
of the girl next to me.
The girl next to me,
who appears to be getting taller,
who appears to be getting older.
My nose catches bacon,
flour, honey, raisin,
and then perfume.
Heavy,
thick,
perfume.
An aroma not to remember.
The door closes,
the footsteps,
resume.

Behind another door,
a cuddle.
Behind another,
a nightmare,
but always the sound of the feet
on the cobbles,
and gravel
and sand
and grass,
from each footstep,
the first to the last.

|||||||

Behind another,
a girl and a mirror.
Another door,
is,
a broken mirror.
Behind another,
a party,
and dirty children's clothes,
there is far too much noise,
in that home.

Eventually,
gradually,
the doors are too far apart to see,
and before us,
a dead end.
Before us,
an end.
I turn to the woman next to me,
and ask "where else can I go?"

"There is no place else to go,
but you can let, go."
"What is your name?" I ask.
"I was daughter once, but I am known by many names,
and you will always be son."

JJJJJJ

"There must be someplace else I can go."
"There is no place else to go, except perhaps,
to let go."
I turn to the darkness ahead and let go of her hand,
and all at once find myself,
on solid land.
There is grass beneath my feet,
the wind is freezing and I am naked,
no clothes on my back,
or shoes on my feet
but there is a sky above me
and perhaps another,
lady to meet.

KKKKKK

A Geometry Of Imagination

I lost myself in the imagination of an empty box. Six stones I was given to play with, smooth of surface and similar in size.

On the first day I tried to play something like Go or Chess and always lost despite giving it my best.

On the second day I tried to make patterns or letters but they never ever seemed clear enough, or to mean much.

On the third day I imagined they were different food, different dishes from different places, but I couldn't taste a thing.

On the fourth day I imagined they were furniture, but I found no space to sit or sleep.

On the fifth day I imagined they were colours and the light in the room shifted, or perhaps it was the smooth surface of my eyes.

On the sixth day I tried to build something but decided I didn't have enough stones.

On the seventh day I gave them names, because I was lonely and had forgotten my own.

They found what was left of me in the imagination of an empty box, what looked like sticks and stones and broken bones but they imagined something else, entirely. The six stones became my headstone, and what I imagined was the shape of me, shimmered unseen before the figures at my grave.

LLLLLL

A woman who exhaled black smoke and spat out watermelon seeds turned to a boy and asked, "what would you do with six stones and an empty box?"

"Four of them I would place on the outside as wheels, one I would use to steer with, and one would become my best friend and together we would ride out of here."

The shape of me shimmered and faded out of my own space. All became blackness and darkness until there was light again, and I found myself in the imagination of another box, completely full of empty people of forgotten names and angular faces. All of us jammed acute and obtuse and tight and taut, between these four corners of empty thought

MMMMMM

NANCY

NNNNNN

Nancy

They found Nancy in the attic, consumed by an armchair, its mould-coloured velvet had imbibed her like forgotten meat would cling wrap. Old curtains of nicotine and lace had been brought forward and draped across her face like a veil, and the only light that found its way into the room, had to penetrate the bone in her skull, ghosts of memories and the stale fabric. The shuffle of the boots on the floorboards gave the dust enough energy to remember how it fell, as it buffered her silhouette in the pale gloom once again. Her skeleton was naked except for a pair of knickers, once black but now greyed with age.

On fully opening the curtains the two men choked on the amount of dust agitated and both squinted as light dawned across the rest of the room. When their eyes adjusted, they were shocked to find another set of footprints that lead directly from the trap door to the chair. It was then they saw that a single, freshly cut rose protruded from the knickers and a clean, white envelope had been placed between her legs, like an offering of some sort. It bore no address, just two words calligraphed in deep blue ink- "For Nancy."

oooooo

For Nancy

I left my dreams behind,
drifting on the inland sea
the memories of the boat,
where you lay next to me.

I left my dreams behind,
trapped between my legs and yours,
consigned to tiny oblivion,
my body and heart in discord.

I left my love behind,
when I chose chastity over ecstasy,
and conformity over the enormity,
of all of you thrust into me.

I left my love behind,
when I listened to the world.
What is under a skirt,
is not what makes a girl.

I left my faith behind,
to be blind only to love.
An agnostic of agapāte,
hearkens the Mourning Dove.
I will leave my kiss behind,
on the pages of our good book,
in the hope that star crossed lovers,
will once again know where to look.

THE LONG ISLAND BUGLE

PASTOR'S SUICIDE LINKED TO DEATH OF TRANSGENDER PROSTITUTE

Residents of Ronkonkoma, Suffolk County, Long Island were left reeling with the discovery of two bodies today that appear to be linked, despite the quite different circumstances.

The body of Pastor Michael Thompson of the Sachem United Methodist Church was discovered on the banks of Lake Ronkonkoma at around 6AM today, near the Beach Club Estate. Initial reports show that the cause of death was suicide by drowning. Pastor Thompson was a widely respected community leader, a winner of numerous Rose growing competitions and an avid supporter of local gardening initiatives.

Across town in an abandoned property on Hauppauge Road, human remains were discovered by two firefighter officers from the nearby Hauppauge fire station. The house appeared to have been broken into and children reported seeing a man who looked like Pastor Thompson on the property looking very distraught. The remains are believed to be those of one Joseph Bristow, known locally as "Nancy," a transgender prostitute who lived in the property but disappeared almost ten years ago, the identity is yet to be confirmed. Prior to her disappearance, Nancy reported several disturbances and cases of harassment to local police. "She had a terrible life, scorned by everyone here but she told me she refused to leave town without her true love," said one former neighbour "she never revealed who that was."

A copy of William Shakespeare's Romeo and Juliet was found with the body of Pastor Thompson. The book is believed to be the original property of Sachem High School Library which both Pastor Thompson and Joseph Bristow attended. They were both members of the creative writing club but were said to have lost contact after graduation, however the Church held annual vigils for Nancy after her disappearance.

John Templeton in New York
Wed 19 May 2021 10.12 EST

QQQQQQ

Of Death And Cherry Blossom

It was spring when I fell in love.
The pink blush on the snow-stained petals
sang of winters passing,
and I found a garden.
Cocooned in silk of cherry suns,
teal clouds and golden dragons,
her marble skin and sable hair steeped into my gaze,
like matcha into clear water.
I drank and became.

In summer she told me her name.
I heard the counting of cicadas,
the salmon song in the streams,
and the rumour of ripe plums.
We shared watermelon behind the walls.
My finger traced the outline of my world,
along the jade and emerald cartography of its skin.
And when I sliced into the sweet pink flesh,
I told her I had found my centre.
She told me she could not leave with me.

In autumn we hid under a pattern of stars,
and the dream compass of a moon.
Its light painted the brown,
crimson and ochre leaves of morning,
into mauve, indigo and other secret shades.
We held hands and her fingers flowed,
like a river between the valleys of mine.

RRRRRR

She passed away in winter with the leaves on the trees.
I found the hands she held me with,
bleeding deep dark red into the famished white snow,
it drank her dry as ice began to settle,
into the tears on her closed eyes,
another spring was always a dream.
My retribution was a typhoon,
an unnatural unmaking undertaking.
I breathed my last breath into the soil I buried her in,
and on that day,
of every winter of every year,
the cherry blossom I became blooms in bursts of blood,
and the wind remembers her tears.

ssssss

A Sociopathic Progression in Four Movements

The First

I burned my dreams again,
and frantically rub the ashes from my eyes,
not for fear of going blind,
but to help me forget them,
because I am here again.
Itching.
Itching under the skin,
the burst of needles from within,
for I am here again.
My heart deceives with each beat,
my pulse but a ripple of a blood drop,
a cicada with no rhythm,
a sound out of time.
There is a tree outside the window,
and its leaves jeer at me in the breeze.
If I could peel the bark from my face,
I may be able to ascertain my age,
and how long I have felt like this,
in this place.
I am here again,
and I predict poor weather today.

TTTTTT

The Second

Snowflakes are unique.
Snowflakes are beautiful.
I have never seen one,
and some have never seen snow.
How many of us have a soul,
if all of us melt in the sun?
We are all born this way,
I like to think,
if I think at all.
Clean,
untouched,
until we melt under the sun,
and become one with the dirt and the rain,
the flooded street and a blocked drain.
Look at all these people,
scurrying around, hurrying around,
as if movement defines a sense of purpose,
a sense of independence,
as if moving,
actually,
makes any sense.
As if any of us,
Actually,
move,
at all.
Stand still,
and the world moves under your feet.
The point you move from,
and the point you wish to move to,
are no longer there already.
Where they were,
and where you were,

are no longer there already.
Tomorrow does not exist,
and the yesterday you remember does not either.
You remember something else,
if you remember at all,
for such is the way of things.

All these people together,
next to each other,
moving from one point to the next,
neither leaving nor arriving.
Talking.
Talking about having nothing to say.
This one.
Look at this one.
She is as bored as the paint on the fucking walls,
and he is the box she is hiding in.
I know that face.
I have seen that face.
She desires intimacy.
She requires intimacy.
The intimacy of bondage,
to be bound,
to be found,
to feel a rope burn her skin.
To feel alive,
and not fucking dead inside.
To be awake,
and not to be here.
And anywhere but,
there.

vvvvvv

The Third

The best place for a mirror,
is an empty room.
Any item of furniture,
has a purpose of its own.
No piece of furniture is ever made,
for any particular room,
and no room is ever constructed,
for a particular piece of furniture,
and the purpose of an empty room,
is not necessarily to be filled.
I stand now before this mirror,
and the mirror,
is the only object in this room,
with a purpose.
I stare into the glass.
I breathe upon the glass.
I see mist upon the glass,
but I see no reflection at all,
and I laugh,
for I have finally found myself.

wwwwww

The Fourth

I break the mirror.
I smash the glass,
not because I am angry,
but because I want to take a piece outside.
I want to take a piece of myself,
outside.
I hold it tightly in my pocket.
It stings on my fingers,
and I know I am awake.
I need it to let me know,
I am awake.
I find her again,
I see her again,
and she sees me,
from the corner of her box.
I show her the glass,
I show her the piece of me,
and she screams.
Is it because she sees nothing?
Or because she sees I am bleeding?
I see the blood,
and I know I am here again,
and as they drag me away,
the piece of me falls to the floor,
and breaks into many more.
I know then,
that I was also there.
In one small piece,
she catches her reflection.
In one small piece,
she catches her reflection.

xxxxxx

The Inkstone

My grandfather gave me a gift,
"An inkstone?" I asked.
"More than that" he replied,
"it's a mirror."
"How is this a mirror?"
"That is a question you must continue to ask of the stone,
and one day you will discover the answer."

It felt cool in my palm,
and peaceful as a winter morning.
I ran my fingers around its simple square shape,
the distance between each point,
a query for my fingers
until the resolution of each corner.

I perceived no reflection in the darkness of the stone,
yet in time I grew to marvel at
how it caught the flicker of any candle in the room,
and the glimmer of the moon,
through any window I designed.

The notion of black is a misconception,
it takes many colours to mix the vagueness of the night,
and the ash of many trees to deepen sumi ink,
so one must be contrite in this sacrifice of light.
A splash of spring water is all I use,
and it is for the water to decide how many drops escape into the recess,
the ink will find them eventually.
I inhale and exhale as I grind the stick back and forth,
and slowly, softly,
the colour of all colours appears.
Slowly,

YYYYYY

softly,
a glimmer of truth appears.
There are ripples of candlelight,
and moonlight on the surface,
seething into being,
such is the way of seeing,
and finding,
a shade of ink.

My mind now steadied and hollow hand readied,
the first dip of my brush,
shatters the dream of the day,
and the wolf hair drinks and drinks deeply.
The smooth rustling scrape across the paper,
sounds like the crush of velvet snow,
or the ruffle of a towel on wet hair,
true perspective is a product of the self,
it is all in the head.
Such sounds,
are all in your head.

Ponderings.
Lines, movements.
Moments.
Pauses.
The shape of questions.
Breathe.
I ask, I look, I write.

zzzzzz

One story begins:
Like a speck of dust in the corner of your vision that you ignore,
there is an empty desk in the corner of the classroom.
And this one ends with my grandfather,
reading all my pages and letters and saying,
"I see who you are now,"
as the last drop of ink,
dries up on the stone.

AAAAAAA

The Man With Black Hole Eyes

If he opens his eyes you will go blind.
Every colour, every tone and hue,
will disappear.
Everything you see,
everything you remember,
will never be here.

Your memories will trace orbital arcs into the vacuum,
of the black holes of his eyes,
and you will bear witness to the unmasking,
of the mortal disguise.

Like the pattern of your iris and the print of your finger,
remnants and shadows of what you were will linger,
upon the event horizon of his brow,
there never was a here or now.

In that final moment you will know the name of ghosts,
the quest for truth will be your undoing,
and the answer will be your unmaking.

This man waits.
This man waits.
This man waits.

BBBBBBB

Blank Canvas

Your fingers felt different on my palm that night, loose of grip and try as I might, I had no perception of bones. A breeze trickled from behind, somewhere behind near where one would find the back or behind of the passageway or hallway and featherly, your fingers fluttered forward as you twirled ahead in the dance and shudder of a dry leaf, a moment or pattern of grief.

"Beyond this door lies a hollow hall and on each wall lie low and high, many a blank canvas from ground to sky, each a memory or moment to discover, an entreated emotion to recover. What you wish to view is entirely up to you just remember, that my heart was and is, never yours to sculpture."

I followed you into the room and lost you in the gloom as a glistening rheum began to form beneath my nose and eyes, and oh did I realise that these lies of sight and sense and corporeal compense began to make no sense at all to my soul in that hollow hall, of seething silence and blank canvas.

You had melted into oils like the retreat of candlewax before the sight of the night, and all the colours and hues of you were now congealed into canvas. The turbulence of teal flowed over your hair, that was once obsidian in our world. The beating crimson I remembered on your lips, now bubbled under every shape and texture of your skin, stretched into an ochre of longing. The line of your limbs and profile of your person now but a shadow across colour, and all those words I now regret, echo infinitely in each strand and stroke of a brush.
With my finger and hand, I reached out to touch, but not unlike the linger of sand, in this rhyme beyond time, I had no perception of bone.

CCCCCCC

It was then that I did resolve, to remove the fabric of my clothes, and reveal the surface of my skin,
naked in the silence seething, to spur my sense of meaning. I will remain here and endure, splinters from the wooden floor, and shudders from the timbers of my limbic limbers, in this hollow hall until I can find, each moment and memory of you,
in each blank, empty, canvas, from ground to sky,
low to high, and finally reveal,
the true colour and shape and hue of you and why,
oh why my idea of love, my oil choked brush stroked image of love, was born to never be enough, and why the bone in your hand,
was the one thing that, I could never truly touch.

DDDDDDD

Salmon Season

Nothing trembled her knees and toes like heroin,
morphine a decent second,
codeine and vodka a distant third,
and I,
was no more than an expired salmon,
limping upstream against a current of craving,
copulative in its delivery and consumptive in its conclusion.
My scales sallow and eyes fallow,
I bore the pungency,
of her shameless addiction,
for there is no room for shame when all is consumed,
just an acrid anxiety,
arachnid and amaurotic.
Her eyes blinkered her mind into a one-way tunnel,
and when I felt romantic,
I saw myself as the light at the end,
that kept drifting further,
and further,
away.
They found her at the side of the river,
and to this day I still cannot bear,
the cold light of a mirror,
and fish markets,
full of dead fish with sunken eyes,
melting into the ice.

EEEEEEE

The Sight Of A Blind Man

Only the blind man could see.
A hundred eyes had the spider on his head,
and his wispy willowy hair was spider thread,
that fluttered in reflection of every sound,
the music of every moment found.
What he could not see he could hear,
what he could not hear he could feel,
and the scent of things was his measure of change.
I asked him what his name was,
and he replied,
"time."
I asked what the spider was,
and he replied,
"your mind."
I asked him what this world was,
and he replied,
"its web."
I asked him how old he was,
and he laughed.
I asked him who I was and all he said was,
"blind."
I asked him what he was,
and he said,
"a lie."
I began to cry until I became thirsty.
I asked him what the thirst was,
and he replied,
"the question."
I asked him what then,
were my tears,
and he replied,
"the answer."

FFFFFFF

The Window

"It's so not fair, I lost my Saturday morning because of you guys, and I don't even smoke," said Olivia, the tallest and most studious of the three girls.

"We were all behind the library together what do you expect?" replied Rachel, the one who wore the most make up and the shortest skirts.

"Yeah Olly, you're such a square. You might as well try a drag now you've done the time," chuckled Emily who then offered up her Marlboro. Emily smoked the most, drank the most and ate the most.

"Eww no thanks, besides mom will kill me. I'm in enough trouble already. *Thank you.*"

"Your mom is ridiculous, she's so extra."

"Super extra," chimed in Rachel.

"She's just been a bit overprotective since my dad left, that's all."

"Well at least she won't be around next weekend," said Emily.

"Um. About that…"

"WHAT?" rang the other two in unison.

"Her trip got cancelled, because of the wildfires or something."

"Shit Olly, what about the party??" exclaimed Rachel.

"I don't know guys."

GGGGGGG

"It's always, always Emily and I, Olly, you've never organised anything. We've invited everybody now."

"I know but come on guys, you know what she's like, there's no way she'd ever let me organise something like that even if our house was a big as either of yours."

"This is why you're still a virgin," proclaimed Rachel.

"Fuck you. I'm a virgin by choice. Besides nobody should consider a serious relationship with anybody until they TRULY know who they are and they WANT out of life."

"Who's talking about serious relationships duh. And which geeky self-help book did you read that in?" prodded Emily.

"Seventeen actually, but you'd probably struggle to read even that."

"WHATEVER!"

"I know what I want anyway," chortled Rachel "Tommy Moore right between my legs!" Emily almost choked on her cigarette and then cackled along.

"Speaking of the devil!" Olivia flung out both her arms to stop her friends dead in their tracks.

"What the hell…" said Rachel as Emily coughed yet again.

"Over there on the corner, it's Tommy Moore and the other guys."

"Shit," said Rachel "we can't talk to them yet, not until we figure out the weekend. This is on you Olly. YOU need to sort this."

HHHHHHH

"Come on then, let's take a detour," said Olivia as she pulled her friends down a side street, "they all give me the creeps anyway."

"What time does the movie start?" Emily asked Olivia.

"We've got plenty of time, at least an hour annnndd we might actually be on time for a change if seeing as we don't have to walk past a certain somebody's favourite boutique."

"HMMPH!" replied the certain somebody in the short skirt.

The cinema was a couple of miles away from school, but the girls normally did not mind the walk across that part of town, as their usual route took them down the main shopping area. There was even a second-hand bookstore that Oliva managed to coax them in to now and again. The direction they now headed in took them across the outskirts of the old residential area. A lot of the properties were empty and run down, the whole place had gone into slow decline since the paper mill closed ten years ago. The newer suburbs on the opposite side of town had boomed over the same period due to significantly better travel connectivity, and the technology park that sprang up on the outskirts. The town was practically split in two, rusted railings and cracked windows on one side, hipsters, and overpriced coffee on the other, a typical contrast of dilapidation and gentrification

"This place sticks out like a sore thumb," said Olivia as she pointed across the street to an ornate wooden one-story building on the corner of Shaw and Harris. In its prime it would not have looked out of place in the French quarter of New Orleans, it was certainly out of place here amongst the surrounding nuclear family style bungalows. The garden was now overgrown, and ivy and other vegetation had begun to lay claim to the blistered paint on the wooden porch and walls.
"It's creepy, doesn't look like anybody has lived there for a while," said Rachel.

Emily lit up another Marlboro and took a drag, "looks kinda cool. If that place is empty, it'd be an awesome place to party."

"You cannot be serious," said Olivia.

"Got any other ideas? Let me see what I can find out about the place, I'll ask my dad. He's already redeveloped a few places on the next block, I wouldn't be surprised if he's checked out this dump already."

Rachel's voice faded away from Olivia's ears and was replaced by a lower octave hum and she felt drawn towards the house again. Her eyes homed in on the small window of the small angle pyramid shaped attic. They were being observed. Olivia froze at the sight of a face in the window and in that moment, she could only hear the hum despite being aware of lip movements on the other girls in the corner of her eyes.

The face of an old woman stared directly into Olivia's eyes with a familiarity that scraped underneath the skin on the back of her neck. Her sallow flesh draped over her skull like an old dust cover and her eyes appeared pitch black from this distance, or it could have been the effect of the dim light in the room she was in. A few seconds later the hum in her ears and the itch in her skin subsided and she turned to speak to her friends.

"Well, that's that, obviously the place isn't empty after all," she still felt unsettled as if under the aftereffects of a strong painkiller.

"What are you talking about?" asked Rachel.

"There's a woman. Right there in the attic."

"Um, where??" asked Emily.

JJJJJJJ

"There up in the attic," Olivia looked again at the window and the woman still looking in her direction, her lips had now creased into a shape that taunted a smile.

"There's nobody there Olly," said a confused Rachel.

"Up there in the damn window!" Olivia turned again to the girls and pointed up towards the attic in frustration.

"Are you feeling okay?" asked Emily, squinting her eyes in confusion and inhaling cigarette smoke as if it would clear up the issue.

"She's right there," Olivia turned again and completely breathless as she observed an empty window " she was in the window."
"Girl. There was nobody. We were both looking at the house we would have seen something," reassured Rachel as she put her arm on Olivia's shoulder and gave Emily a bemused look "come on let's get to this movie."

The face of the old woman lingered in Olivia's head, lingered like a watermark and long enough for her to not fully pay attention to the images on the screen. The movie began and ended and eventually all the images of the day began to subside. Nothing came to her mind over dinner, and she got an earful from her mother about the detention. All her responses were automated yet relatively successful.

From her bedroom window she had a substantial view of the east side of town, the west side was mostly hilly. The more affluent properties, where Emily and Rachel lived were set even higher up in the hills. That is how it was in this town and many others; people look down upon some others who look down upon more and the people on the bottom only ever look at the ground. Olivia could not see the old house clearly, but she could make out the implied silhouette of the street. There were

KKKKKKK

less streetlights in that part of town and those that were there flickered an unhealthy shade.

She preferred the view of the town at night, in fact she preferred any view at night. Her mind engaged and imagined more, with a lack of detail, the moments of the day were wiped clean and this town or any town could be something else for a time. She could be somewhere else for a time, the trees now dark clouds of fog, the car lights fireflies, and the sky a porous mauve, the colour of dreams and the sparkle in the stars- a wish that perhaps her dreams would one day become reality. Perhaps one day she would open her eyes to an altogether different day.

As she gazed, she became aware of her clouded reflection in the window, misted outlines of her shape splattered with the lights and movement from outside. Like the town now, this image of her was intrinsically different to what she saw in the daytime. It was a hint of Olivia, an abstract, and as she studied it more, she thought perhaps she may be able to see her true form, her true self. It was then she recalled the face of the woman. Olivia wondered if perhaps the woman was looking at her or also examining her own reflection. This train of thought ended abruptly with the rattle of her phone as it vibrated on her desk. A message in her group chat from Rachel.

R- GUURRRLS IT'S ON! THE OLD MAN SAYS THAT PLACE HAS BEEN EMPTY FOR LIKE 20 YEARS. IT'S OWNED BY SOME TRUST OR TRUSTY THING WHATEVER THAT IS THAT WON'T SELL.

O- NO WAY. I SAW SOMEBODY THERE. THERE WAS A WOMAN IN THE HOUSE.

R- SERIOUSLY! THERE WAS NOBODY OLLY.

E- MAYBE SHE SAW A GHOST HAHA

LLLLLLL

O-NOT FUNNY!!

R- WE'RE SCOPING IT OUT TOMORROW BEFORE WE GET BACK TO SCHOOL. IF IT'S COOL WE JUST TELL EVERYBODY WE'VE CHANGED VENUE.

O- NO WAY.

R- YES WAY.

E- COME ON OLLY, DON'T BE SCARED WE'LL BE WITH YOU!

R- IT'S ON. I'M PICKING YOU BOTH UP TOMORROW. I GOT THE CAR BACK, PUNISHMENT OVER.

O- I DON'T LIKE THIS...

E- CHILL...

R- YA, CHILL...

The house looked the same as yesterday and all the windows were empty. Olivia scanned and scanned the attic window but could make out nothing within.

"See. Nothing. Nobody," said Rachel.

"So how are we doing this?" asked Olivia.

"You, are going to find a way inside and open the door for us."

"What the hell! Why me??"

MMMMMMM

"Because Olly dear, you're the party host and sorting out the replacement venue is your responsibility."

"Fuck you!" she replied as she turned to Emily for support, who just shrugged her shoulders and lit up a cigarette.

"If anything happens to me in there, it's all on you."

"The place is empty as girl, come on, sooner you get us in, sooner we can check this place out."

Olivia approached the house, the grass on the lawn, was thick but dried out in places and littered with remnants of weeds. She approached slowly and kept one eye on the attic window, but no face appeared. Behind the grime she could just make out the shape of drawn curtains on the ground floor. There were no obvious signs of entry from the front, unless she broke some glass but that could raise attention, despite the street and other homes appearing quite deserted. She turned to the girls on the pavement and raised her hands for a suggestion, Rachel waved for her to head towards the rear of the house.

The yard was overgrown completely, like a scene from the apocalypse movie they saw the day before. There was a fountain full of moss and dirt and a faded cherub with broken wings in the centre. The rear of the house looked quite similar to the front, an overgrown porch and to the left a conservatory, the glass opaque with the nicotine colour of age and abandonment. Her eyes squinted and she made out a space in the doorframe, a slight aperture, it was open. She swallowed a hard lump of nothing and approached slower than she did earlier, the wood on the rear porch creaked yet felt like sponge under her feet. The door was open slightly, there was an opening but judging by the moss and dirt around the doorframe it had not moved from that position in quite some time.

NNNNNNN

Olivia peered inside but could only perceive empty darkness and barely the frame of a house. She inhaled slightly and caught stale air but no other scent of malevolence. The hinges had seized up over the years and so the door wouldn't budge at first. She gave it a hard shove, and then another and then another and almost fell over as the door crashed to the floor in a chorus of dust, the frame itself gave way, the wood completely rotten.

Ahead she could make out a hallway, dimly illuminated by the light coming through the glass in the front door. It was completely bare, wooden floorboards and doors on either side and a banister rail opposite the front door which indicated a stairway. She decided if she couldn't open the door, she would get the girls to come around the back and began to creep inside. When she did, she was overcome by silence, complete and utter silence. She could hear nothing, not the even the breath in her lungs or the pulse in her temples. She looked down at her feet padding across the wooden floor, saw her legs moving, but could not hear them. As she approached the front door the staircase to her right came into view, and as it did a hum rose from her eardrums, the same hum that she heard the day before.

It was a greeting, a beckoning, and her skin began to itch again and as it did somehow, in some way, she felt it would only go away if she went upstairs, she had to go and see. She could not explain to herself why, she could not formulate an alternative course of action, she could not hear her own thoughts. In this mood of mental muteness, she silently made her way up the stairs, up to the first floor, the space that was the attic. It was dimly lit by the one window ahead and one behind. It was empty, completely empty, and square. As she motioned towards the window she became away of the point, the centre of the pyramidal roof above her and the humming subsided. She paused to gather her thoughts and look around, the humming had gone but she was still blanketed in silence, as if she were in an old temple or cathedral hall.

OOOOOOO

Oliva approached the window to see if the girls were there and call out to them, as she did the frame of light coming into the room drew her further and as she approached the glass every inch of her flesh burned with a scream of pins under her skin. She could not move, her whole being had been slammed into the spot, into the space behind the window and in the glass, she saw not her own reflection, but that of the old woman. The only action that her body allowed was that of single tear forming in her right eye. For a fraction of a second, its coolness crept down her cheek and brought her brief respite from the burning under her skin, which returned twofold when beyond the horrid reflection, she saw Emily and Rachel outside on the street and herself standing behind them.

PPPPPPP

Life Is A Square Hole On The Floor

YOU are deep in the throb and clog of the artery in my neck,
the one I wish to sever to detach myself from this place of transfusion.
It is fitting that the taste on YOUR tongue,
and the image on YOUR lens are fabrications,
YOUR own creations.
YOU exist in the senses and what YOU experience may not be objective,
but YOU experience things and so THEY are real,
nonetheless.
With all this in mind,
so to speak and in some sense,
nonetheless and less is more or more and more,
and the relativity of binary all become senseless,
and, none sense.
Occasionally I find lucidity in dreams and letters.
Occasionally I dream of letters and occasionally, lucidity,
creates authenticity and perhaps,
I have created or been created.
Perhaps creation is just another matter of perspective.

"YOU are the universe," THEY sing to you,
and THEY were absolutely correct,
although THIS is not what THEY meant.

In another language YOU could be I or I could be YOU and THEY could be someone or nobody or nothing at all.

If I severed this artery, and bled deep crimson, how long would this image remain with YOU? How would the room smell?
What sound would YOU make?

If I used a fountain pen,
would all of THIS be more dramatic in effect?

QQQQQQQ

If I did not bleed at all,
would the mystery remain with YOU forever?

All of THIS, would be relative to YOU,
what I write is just a theory of I.

If I could write in a language YOU could not read, all of this would make less sense,
in some sense,
it would not exist,
and perhaps I would not exist.
WE claim to speak the same language but, YOU will always see what YOU SEE,
as will I.

And so only occasionally do I find lucidity,
in dreams and letters,
but always,
always,
there is this square hole on the floor.

RRRRRRR

Shapeshifters

Everybody looked strange in the park that day, I felt as though I was a weed that nobody came there to see but noticed anyway. The girl who sulked on the swing, her mother with the fake smile, the couple with the dirty poodle and the lad who appeared to tell jokes to a can of beer telepathically, all of them. All of them seemed to be looking at me. Me, minding my own business minding them not mind their business, alone on the end of this old park bench, in the centre of which is a plaque in memory of somebody I do not care enough about to read about.

I wondered why I stood out, why I seemed odd to them. Perhaps it was because I was alone, and they were not for even that lad had a can of beer for company. Perhaps it was because I felt lonely and perhaps, they sensed it in much the same way animals sense the arrival of spring. Perhaps I was imagining all of this, but one fact was undoubtedly clear, I was alone, and I felt terribly alone. I had not had physical contact with another human being for almost ten years, any meaningful contact that is.

I cannot count the moment some months back when the young lady in the convenience store accidentally stroked my palm as she passed me my change. The shock, almost electrical was too much for me to bear and I dropped my change on the floor as I bolted out of the place. I can still see the look of alarm in her burning blue eyes when I close mine sometimes. This is what ten years does to a man, perhaps this is how the world looks to a man after ten such years or how the world looks at a man, who has not been touched in ten years. I felt their gaze more than I felt the sun and my skin began to recall how it felt that day in the convenience store, in the aftermath and awkward come down of a touch of a hand. I knew then that it was time to go home.

Dinner was a microwaved chicken katsu and rice from another convenience store. My stomach now paid the price of my shame these

SSSSSSS

days, they had pork katsu in the other store I used to go to, but I had now shamed myself into chicken. Shame is a powerful concept. People write about it often, but no words make you feel it more than an empty or unsatisfied stomach, but that is probably something else to write about entirely. My abdomen was distended enough to make me aware of my breathing but not feel completely full. I do not like to hear my breath entering and leaving my body on such occasions, it feels like the ticking of a clock and sounds completely different to how it did that moment ten years ago, vocal, profound and alive.

I rolled onto to my back and lay with the disposable chopsticks in my hands. I pressed them together at the seam, knowing full well that they would not stick together again, that my hunger had torn them apart permanently and forever. Such things are a habit for men such as I. Eventually I exhaled my stomach away and regained the ability to use my legs which carried me to the fridge in the corner of the room, from which I took a can of beer, and then over to my desk and computer in the other corner.

I looked for a movie to watch but could not find anything interesting enough. I checked out some porn but could not find anything exciting enough. I had settled on chicken for dinner, so I needed something else to be more than enough. Almost two hours had gone by, more time wasted and much less achieved and in bored desperation I found myself trawling through internet classified ads in the personals section as I often did. You can find more about people in such places than you can staring at them in the park sometimes.

There did not seem to be anything unusual on the menu that night, all pretty standard fare and nothing peculiar, in this context at least.

> *Looking for casual first meet*
> *27 years*
> *chubby 27yo guy, shy, clean. Looking for first casual meet.*

TTTTTTT

> *Suck you on the docks*
> *24 years*
> *Come and get sucked by docks today, safe, discreet, lob it in my mouth.*

> *Male looking ladies and couple*
> *23 years*
> *I am in the city today if any ladies or couples need massage skills. Can travel. I have 8 inches, can send pic.*

> *Couple 29M and 25F seeking fun with female*
> *29 years*
> *Young couple seeking female, ideally 25-40 for relaxed fun. Genuine, friendly, looking for new experiences!*

Just as I was about to acknowledge that I was beginning to feel hungry again and get agitated, the next advertisement blew up my stomach and I became aware of my breathing for the second time that day.

> *Full body no contact massage*
> *19 years*
> *World first NCBBM. Completely safe. Completely sensual. Be touched and not touched until you can't touch anything else.*

I was intrigued. NCBBM? I'd never heard of it, I was familiar with all the usual red-light acronyms like CIM, BJ, BBBJ and BBM- bare body massage. No contact bare body massage was what I could only assume it stood for based on the rest of the description. It sounded almost like an oxymoron and the notion of being touched and not touched, did in fact turn me on. I was now hungry but did not want anything to eat. I picked up my phone and called the number that was on the screen.

UUUUUUU

"Fuseijitsu Massage, how may we be of service?" chirped a young ladies voice.

"I'd like to book a no, no contact?"

"No contact bare body massage?"

"Yes, a no contact bare body massage."

"Or course sir, when would you like to come?"

"How does that work exactly? Does she wear a body suit or something?"

"Ah is it your first-time sir?"

"Yes, this will be my first time, I just wondered how it works."

"It's a membrane massage sir."

"A membrane massage?"

"Yes sir. The first one in the world. Completely original. Completely safe. Completely sensual."

"What does it entail?"

"With all due respect sir, some things cannot be explained, only experienced. I guarantee you will not be disappointed."

"But what if.."

"We also give an introductory fifty percent discount on your first visit sir" she interrupted.

vvvvvvv

"Oh. Ok then."

"When would you like to come sir?"

"In around an hour or so."

"Can I put you down for ten thirty?"

"Yes, that's fine thank you."

"And which girl do you wish to book?"

"Oh, I'm not sure, can I choose when I get there?"

"I'm sorry sir no, all bookings must be made in advance."

"Ok do you have a website where I can check them out or something?"

"I'm afraid not sir, just tell me the name of a girl you would like to book."

"But I don't know what they look like."

"This is not about what you see sir, but what you feel. Just let me know the name of a girl you would like to book. I promise you will not be disappointed. If there is anything to your dissatisfaction, I guarantee a full refund and a complimentary session."

"But.."

"Just a name sir."

"Sabrina" I said the only name I could think of. The only name that had been on my mind for the last ten years.

wwwwwww

"Sabrina. Perfect, we shall see you shortly sir."

"Don't you need my name or any other details?"

"No sir just let me know the name of the girl you have booked on arrival. Goodbye."

Slightly bewildered I put down my phone and read over the advert again, mouthing the words with my lips as I did. I had apparently booked a membrane massage with Sabrina which apparently, I would not regret. This thought stuck in my mind like a bee sting while I freshened up.

I found Fuseijitsu Massage at the end of an alley after walking past a wine bar, a karaoke pub and a twenty-four-hour laundrette. A pink neon sign about the size of a mailbox, stuttering in the centre of a large blacked out window was the only indication that I had found the right place. The brick exterior had been painted black up to what I imagined would be another floor. The only entrance was a large heavy duty steel door, also painted a thick black. Above it was a battered old CCTV camera and to the right on the wall was a haggard buzzer. I pressed the grey button twice but heard no sound, on my third attempt a click informed me that door had been unlocked and so I opened it with some effort and a held breath.

I descended about five or six narrow steps into a small dimly lit waiting area. On either side of me were two well-worn dark grey or black leather sofas. In front was a wide and deep-set mahogany effect countertop, behind which sat a very thin Chinese girl and behind her was door. She looked up at me from behind her extremely thick glasses and called me forward. I initially could not make out her eyes for the reflection of what I discovered was an iPad on the countertop.

XXXXXXX

Something about her felt out of place in her tiny, frayed denim shorts and baggy grey tee, and the hair tied back in a bun as if she did not have time to wash it, this image was not what I expected. She was also I lot prettier than I expected. She did not say anything at first but beckoned me closer still until my stomach was in contact with the countertop and I could smell her hair, which smelt of the weather outside. It was then that I noticed the iPad, she was sketching on it. I had just enough time to make out a picture of woman bound with course rope and shaded in various neon colours before she spoke to me.

"Name?"

"Oh. Erm. Yes. I have a booking for Sabrina."

"Ah yes sir" she replied as she promptly stood to attention and pointed to the door behind her "this way please." She opened the door, and I entered a small corridor as the sound of her flip flops followed behind "take the next door on the right sir." I then found myself in a changing room very much like the type you find in public bath houses, small tiles, lockers and wooden benching. There were four shower cubicles in front of me. She took clean towels and a pair of flip flops from a shelf on the wall and placed them on the bench beside me. From a cardboard box underneath the bench she pulled out a large dispenser bottle and placed that on the bench also.

"Lockers are provided for your belongings sir; you can set the lock electronically to any combination you require. They are quite safe. Please shower thoroughly, your hygiene and safety are important to us. You will find any toiletries you need in the shower cubicles. Once you have showered please rub generous amounts of oil onto every inch of your skin."

"Oil?" I asked as a glanced at the dispenser on the bench.

YYYYYYY

"It is our own unique blend of essential oils, formulated to heighten your senses and to intensify the overall experience. You will find more in the membrane room, but we encourage you to use as much as possible. We encourage you to experience as much as possible. I will wait outside sir, once you are ready please cover yourself with a towel, call me and I will take you to the membrane room." She left me as I contemplated the notion of an oil heightening my senses, was it some kind of narcotic or some form of hocus pocus? I was about to find out shortly regardless. I did as I was instructed, and she led me down the end of the hallway to another door as I watched the backs of her knees point to each other as she walked. For a moment I imagined feeling the silk of them and her legs floating around me and she turned to look me straight in the eyes.

"There are no time limits in the membrane room, the only limitations are your senses. You can only enter the membrane room naked, and you cannot take any foreign bodies inside. Please leave your sandals here, I will leave a fresh towel on the hook on the wall for you, please shower afterwards" she said to me as she held out her hand. I looked at her confused.

"I must ensure that you are naked when you enter the room and are not taking any foreign bodies inside. Your towel please sir." I blushed as I handed her my towel, I did not realise I had an erection. She did not look at it directly, but I could tell by her smile that she was aware of it. She opened the door, I entered. She closed the door, and I heard her flip flops fade away down the hall.

I was in a dark room, padded from floor to ceiling in what felt like cushioned latex, the whole room appeared to be lubricated with the same oil that my skin was, it smelt like the hair on the Chinese girl, like the weather outside. My eyes squinted at first until a dim light appeared and began to glow in the centre of the room. As my eyes adjusted, I could see that the room was circular and perhaps ten feet in diameter,

ZZZZZZZ

completely padded and completely lubricated. The oil cast a black shimmer across the place when it caught the light.

The source of the light stole the air from my lungs, the unexpected and yet expected surprise of it all. The unexpected expectations of a night in pursuit of a no contact bare body massage. An oxymoron of evenings, a light in a dark room, a darkness in a light in the centre of the room. In the centre of the room from the floor to the ceiling was a cylindrical chamber and in the light of which I could make out a shape, the silhouette, the shadow and form of a woman.

"Sabrina?"

"Yes" replied a voice that I did not recognise but felt I knew "come to me" she said. I took a step forward and instantly slipped and fell on my back. She giggled and the sound tickled my ears and skin.

"It's okay" she said "nothing matters in here; you can't hurt yourself. Come to me anyway you feel like. Just feel as you do. Feel me when you do."

I was reluctant to try and stand up again, so I half crawled, half slid towards her, like a baby would towards its mother. And it felt completely fine doing so, in fact it warmed and soothed every inch of me, my skin, the oil, the padding, all encapsulated me in amniotic bliss. My forehead slid forward an inch into the cylinder and it welcomed my head as it I did. It was not hard, it was not some form of glass or plastic but rather a thin, silky membrane like a contraceptive sheath, and she was inside. Sabrina was inside and all around us was the oil, as omnipresent as the air in our lungs and thick like fog.

"Touch me," she said "feel me. Hold me," she said. And so, I did. I managed to wobble to my feet and embrace her through my skin, the oil, the membrane and more oil to her skin. All the way through my

AAAAAAAA

memories and my imagination I felt her. I felt her. I touched her. And she felt wonderful. She was wonderful. I have no idea how long I spent in that room with her. Wriggling. Writhing. Sweating. Secreting. Blending. Bonding. I went mad in there and came back again. I went away in there and fell over again and again.

"I have to go now" she finally said "I have to rest and be myself again. Goodbye my love." The room went dark and when I managed to catch my breath I wriggled around until I found the door and the way outside. I found the flip flops and the fresh towel and took an age to get back to the shower room. I took longer still to wash myself and just as long to remember the combination to my locker. It seemed like a lifetime ago when I was last there, placing all my possessions neatly inside a small square, like we all feel compelled to do so often.

"Was it to your satisfaction sir?" asked the Chinese girl with the same smile she wore when I saw her last.

"Yes, it was. She was, completely."

"I had no doubt she would be."

"You were right, completely. How much do I owe?"

"Ah yes the bill sir" she replied as she held out her hand, her palm facing upwards.

"I'm sorry how much is it?"

"Your hand sir."

"I'm sorry?"

BBBBBBBB

"Please give me your hand sir," her reply was firm. I reached out with my hand and instinctively closed my eyes, for a moment I saw the blue eyes of the girl in the convenience store and a cold snap danced down my spine. When I opened them, my hand was in the hand of the Chinese girl who now looked at me with a familiar smile and my reflection in her eyes. "Come back as many times as you wish sir. Feel as much as you wish sir. And when you learn the value of such feelings you will know the price you have to pay. If you do not learn the value of such feelings, there will be a price to pay regardless." The sensation in my palm told me there was no reply to give and no questions to ask. It was time for me to leave and so I did.

Over the next few weeks, I went back many times. I saw many pictures of bound ladies sketched on the iPad, I saw that smile many times. I had many erections and I drowned in oil and I hardly spoke a word to Sabrina. It drove me to delirium each time. Was it Sabrina? Was it really her? Who was Sabrina? I could hardly remember her; did I even know a Sabrina? All I knew in those weeks was ecstasy and greed and feelings of skin and time became as viscous as the oil I breathed. I did not stop. I did not pause. I did not breathe; I did not ask any questions of myself. In the end I only wanted to know one thing. What did she look like? What did this Sabrina look like? What did my Sabrina look like?

The first chain of what could be considered some sort of a logical thought process that I had in those weeks was how I could get to see what she looked like. I had to enter the room naked, this I knew. I had also spent enough time lost in that membrane to know that despite its tactility, I could not tear it with my bare hands. I had to cut it. I had to find a way to cut it open and figure out a way to get a knife or something suitable into that room without the Chinese girl knowing. Something about her was dangerous, there must have been a particularly good reason why a girl that skinny could smile so confidently on her own in such an establishment. There were probably many reasons.

CCCCCCCC

I found the answer to my problem in the membrane itself. The answer was a contraceptive sheath. I placed a Swiss Army Knife inside a condom and tied it shut. With much trepidation and plenty of lubrication I managed to conceal it in my rectum and paid Fuseijitsu Massage another visit.

"Do you want to feel me again?" asked the shadow I called Sabrina.

"I want to feel you always" I replied as I wriggled around her.

"Always?" she asked.

"Always. I want to feel you always. And I want more."

"What more is there?" she gasped.

"I want to see you." I panted.

"You can't see me yet."

"Why not? I must see you."

"You haven't determined my value yet."

"I must see you. I must have you. All of you."

"You know not my value."

"My desire should be value enough" as I thrust my arm into my posterior, tore open my concealment with my teeth like a ferocious beast to reveal a steal blade that shimmered like the oil.

"What are you doing?" she asked.

DDDDDDDD

"It's okay I just want to see you" I replied.

"No!"

"It's okay."

"No! No! It's not. Please!"

I sliced downwards into the membrane and tore it apart like a spoiled child would open a gift on a birthday and gazed upon her. She was not as I imagined. She was not the Sabrina I thought I could remember. She was not the Sabrina I imagined her to be. She was slimmer than her shadow suggested, and her skin was not as smooth as the oil suggested. A scar on her cheek led me to a discoloured eye that saw more than I could imagine in a second, it saw all of me, through me and within me and it burned me with my own reflection. Before I could figure out how to breathe a sharp pain exploded in the back of my head and my eyes closed like those of a foetus.

"Who the hell is this guy?" asked the Chinese girl as she dragged my body out into the alley and nimbly flicked it into the trunk of a black Toyota.

"No idea" replied Sabrina as she inhaled a cigarette and the scar on her face disappeared. When she exhaled the smoke, her eyes blended to the colour of the weather outside and she continued with her social commentary, "turned out to be just another wanker."

EEEEEEEE

A Saab in the Snow

I came up to the mountain for peace,
to not hear a hum when I closed my eyes,
and not taste sin on the air in the morning.
Nobody gets down from here in winter,
and nobody bothers you until spring.
No TV, no internet,
and just one jazz station,
crackling through the snow,
The wind and splats on the glass,
echo the snare drums when the timing is right.
You won't know this place,
but when I do go outside,
I like to stand on the old railway bridge,
over the frozen river.
I like to think about slow fish,
and the rust on the steel,
sleeping under the white blanket,
until it will blossom in the spring.
I get ideas and go back and write,
about where I came from,
and where I want to go,
about who I used to be,
who I want to be,
and all the people in between and sometimes,
there is a story I can read.

FFFFFFFF

For five minutes a piano and a trumpet took me on a ride,
like an old SAAB on a back road gliding,
from one side to the other side,
and then the news jingle told me it was time to quit,
and pour a glass and think about all of it.

Four children found a body inside a snowman,
they hadn't seen him before but his red carrot of a nose,
came from the farm in the valley.
Red carrots are rarer things and real snowmen rarer still.
I then heard a screech and a crash outside and rushed to the window,
as the snowman melted in my ears like sorrow.

It was dark but I saw a shape and a mess against the old tree,
and two twisted headlight beams making shadows,
and fireflies of the snow.
I went out to look for a driver and was saddened to recognise,
the shape of an old SAAB.
They don't make them anymore,
they won't make anymore
and this one,
was no more.

I found her leant against the trunk,
staring at the ground and not wanting to be found.
In the dim light when she inhaled her cigarette,
I thought I could make out the colour of her eyes,
just for a moment,
brown then green,
just for a moment green,
and then brown.

GGGGGGGG

"Are you ok?"
"Do you think anybody ever feels alive when they are born?"
"I'm sorry…"
"Don't be, nobody asked to be here."
"Are you hurt in anyway?"
"I'm fine, I just forgot my glasses."
"I see."
"You'd see more you know, if the sky wasn't there,"
she said as she pointed her cigarette upwards like a flare.
"If the sky wasn't there?"
"If the sky wasn't there, you would see more.
It's just there to limit your field of vision."
"Are you sure you're ok?"
"I'm fine."
"Where did you come from?"
"That's an old story."
"Where were you going?"
"That's a new one."
"Do you want to come inside? We can call for help."
"No, it's fine, I don't think I have far to go. I can walk."
"It's freezing it's too dangerous."
"No less dangerous than driving tonight.
I can walk, the ground is here to give my feet something to walk on."
"I can't let you go like this; you don't even have your glasses like you said."
"I don't need them; I realised all glass is made from the crystals dreams left behind."
"What?"
"All glass, spectacles, windows, mirrors. What do you do?"
"I'm a writer, you?"
"I'm just another story, you should go back inside and write another. Thank you."
"What's your name?"
"You'll find out soon enough."

                HHHHHHH

"I'm ****"
"What?"
"I'm ****"
"Nice to meet you. You don't say it loud enough."
"Say what?"
"Your name. Do you know why?"
"I've never noticed, but people often forget my name after they meet me."
"That's because it's probably the one word you have no definition for. I'm sure they never forget your face though."
"Why do you say that?"
"Because your expressions will remind them of something they forgot, perhaps your stories do too.
Now,
I must say goodbye."

She turned towards the wind and snow,
and with one last blow,
her cigarette smoke wafted into my lungs,
and just for second,
it felt like it belonged.
The crunch under my soles,
reminded me of the ground,
that was there for my feet to walk upon,
and in that moment I found,
a sound and a murmur of my soul.

||||||||

Back inside the room I felt cold,
and just for a second slow,
I imagined having something to hold,
a person, a body or even a figure made of snow.
The news still spoke of the melted snowman,
the carrot, his coal lump buttons on the floor,
and the steel rimmed glasses he wore.
Then the music started again,
and I began to write again.

Epilogue

"The Gospel of Déjà Vu," or
"How To Write Fiction."

I am an omnipresence of imaginings.
In your perception of a moment,
I am the future, the past,
and in the mind of who I imagine,
and in the mind of those who find them.
In your perception of a moment,
all this time,
and all of you,
and all of them,
are also in my mind.
There is no god because I did not write him,
and I am not here because he did not read me.
There is no written word that has not been spoken,
but not all that is spoken is written,
and so it will always and never be,
you feel me?

KKKKKKKK

For The Reader

there is beauty
close your eyes
          listen

there is beauty
open your eyes
          breathe

there is beauty
open your hands
          touch

there is beauty
close your hands
          hold

there is beauty
in the eyes of the blind
there is beauty
smile for the deprived

in the reflection of light in every drop of rain
in winter morning mist shapes from your mouth
in the scent of open coffee jars and the night lights of cars
in sleep in dreams in the sound of streams
in your name greeted
in a heart not cheated
  in love
   in love
    in love
in being alone
in being at home

          LLLLLLL

in having a home
in having a moment
to call home

there is beauty in this world
there is you
there is you

MMMMMMMM

https://www.instagram.com/juxtaproser/

NNNNNNNN